President Kennedy created the Peace Corps to, among other things, instill a sense of purpose in the lives of young people. William Hershey shows how his time in the Corps not only changed his life but gave him a valuable international perspective that he brought to his long, successful career as a top political journalist.
—Larry J. Sabato, author of "The Kennedy Half-Century" and director of the Center for Politics at the University of Virginia

A first-class journalist, Bill Hershey's memoir of his Peace Corps experiences in Ethiopia speaks eloquently for the contributions of hundreds of thousands of volunteers who made a difference for their fellow human beings across the globe.
—Michael F. Curtin, former editor and associate publisher, The Columbus Dispatch and coauthor of "The Ohio Politics Almanac"

Bill Hershey, like millions of men of his generation, was not keen on being drafted to serve in the jungles of Vietnam. For that reason and an interest in the Kennedy-era Peace Corps, Bill landed in Ethiopia as a volunteer who was immediately faced with stark poverty and cultural differences. Bill's latest book includes a series of interesting, insightful and entertaining columns and articles he wrote over a 50-year span. That is the same 50-year span that started with the idealism and call to service inspired by President Kennedy and ended with the America-first and xenophobia of President Trump. Bill's columns and articles expertly span those eras in a series of personal experiences peppered with his professional experience as a political columnist and writer.
—Mary Anne Sharkey, former politics and opinion editor at The Plain Dealer, and fellow, Institute of Politics, Harvard University

Taking the Plunge into Ethiopia

Tales of a Peace Corps Volunteer

WILLIAM HERSHEY

The University of Akron Press
Akron, Ohio

All inquiries and permission requests should be addressed to the Publisher, The University of Akron Press, Akron, Ohio 44325-1703.

ISBN: 978-1-62922-266-0 (paper)
ISBN: 978-1-62922-267-7 (ePDF)
ISBN: 978-1-62922-268-4 (ePub)

A catalog record for this title is available from the Library of Congress.

∞ The paper used in this publication meets the minimum requirements of ANSI / NISO Z39.48–1992 (Permanence of Paper).

Cover photo: Gondar Castle by William Hershey. These buildings in Gondar, dating to the 17th century and Emperor Fasilides, are part of the fortress city of Fasil Ghebbi, a UNESCO World Heritage Site. The fortress city includes palaces, churches, monasteries, and other public and private buildings. Fasil Ghebbi served as the center of Ethiopian government from 1636 to 1864.
Cover design: Amy Freels

All photos appear courtesy of William and Marcia Hershey

Taking the Plunge into Ethiopia was typeset in Minion Pro by Amy Freels. It was printed on sixty-pound natural and bound by Bookmasters of Ashland, Ohio.

To the people of Dabat, Ethiopia, who welcomed a stranger
into their lives and trusted him to teach their children

Contents

Preface

JOHN C. GREEN

IN OUR PRESENT era of highly polarized politics, the Peace Corps is a rare agency that draws bipartisan support—and has since its founding in the early 1960s. For evidence of this fact, one needs to look no further than the forewords to this book by two former governors of Ohio: Democrat Richard F. Celeste (Peace Corps director, 1979–81) and Republican Bob Taft (Peace Corps volunteer, Tanganyika/Tanzania 1963–65).

William Hershey's "Taking the Plunge into Ethiopia: Tales of a Peace Corps Volunteer" is a welcome addition to the Bliss Institute's book series, showing that politics doesn't just generate conflict but can also produce consensus. Indeed, the Peace Corps is a fascinating example of the latter: Governor Celeste describes how a volunteer felt that service provided her with "the gift of new eyes," while Governor Taft notes how it has created "more vibrant communities across the world." One reason for this broad political support for the

Peace Corps is that it embodies a key element of the uniquely American "spirit": the tradition of volunteering to help disadvantaged people help themselves. This tradition is at once individualistic and communal, self-actualizing as well as sacrificial, decentralized but highly organized. It has the potential to transform both the volunteers and those assisted.

This tradition is the backbone of the vast array of civic associations in the United States that populate an "independent sector" that operates alongside the private and public sectors. These sectors overlap in many ways, often in the form of partnerships, of which the Peace Corps and its domestic counterparts, such as AmeriCorps, are just one example.

Another reason for the Peace Corps' broad political support is its success. Although not without criticism and controversies, it has largely met its three original goals:

- To help the people of interested countries in meeting their needs for trained workers;
- To help promote a better understanding of Americans on the part of the peoples served;
- To help promote a better understanding of other peoples on the part of Americans.

This book is part of the third goal, "to bring the world back home," and is part of a large and growing literature by current and returned Peace Corps volunteers. This literature is documented on the Peace Corps Worldwide website (https://peacecorpsworldwide.org/), an affiliate of the National Peace Corps Association (NPCA), a private advocacy group for the agency as well as current and returned volunteers. The website is an outgrowth of the Peace Corps

Writers project that began in 1989. In keeping with the Peace Corps ethos, the website is managed by volunteers, proclaiming that "No one needs to join, but everyone can belong."

The website lists more than 700 Peace Corps alumni authors, indexed by name, location of service, and year of their publications. Memoirs of the authors' in-country experiences are the most common genre, but these writings vary enormously in style, including narratives, reflections, analyses, short stories, and poetry. Also included are books by authors with a Peace Corps background on a variety of topics. Most of the authors have one publication, but some authors—particularly in the last category—have multiple books to their credit. Service in nearly 90 countries and regions is reflected in these publications. (Many works were published under the Peace Corps Writers Imprint and are available through Amazon.com).

The genre of "Taking the Plunge into Ethiopia" is journalism, with the 12 main essays originally published in daily newspapers, some as longer magazine pieces and others as shorter columns. Along with an introduction, these essays memorialize Hershey's experiences as a Peace Corps volunteer, vividly capturing insights he gained from his service. In addition, he uses these insights to better understand the United States and its place in the world. The afterwords by Kathleen Coskran, a Peace Corps volunteer with comparable service, and Abebe Kirkos, one of Hershey's Ethiopian students, help put Hershey's experiences in perspective.

Hershey's service occurred during the late 1960s in Ethiopia, which was among the initial countries to accept Peace

Corps volunteers. This book is in good company: works by
some three dozen returned Ethiopian volunteers are listed
with Peace Corps Worldwide. The number and scope of these
offerings may reveal a special bond between the volunteers
and Ethiopia. But it could be that similar bonds developed
between all volunteers and the countries where they served.
(Hershey also provides a brief background essay on Ethiopia's
history and culture.)

Still another reason for Peace Corps' broad support is the
strong community created by the program. It is anchored in
the quarter-million returned volunteers, many of whom went
on to have impressive careers. Just a few examples include:

- Tony Hall (Thailand 1966–1967), Ohio Democratic
  congressman, U.S. ambassador to the United
  Nations Agencies for Food and Agriculture
- Tom Petri (Somalia 1966–1967), Wisconsin
  Republican congressman, honorary Officer of the
  Most Excellent Order of the British Empire
- Ken Hackett (Ghana 1968–1971), president of
  Catholic Relief Services, U.S. ambassador to the
  Vatican
- M. Peter McPherson (Peru 1965–1966), USAID
  administrator, president emeritus of the Association
  of Public and Land-grant Universities
- Drew S. Days III (Honduras 1967–1969), U.S.
  solicitor general
- Reed Hastings (Swaziland 1983–1985), co-founder
  and CEO of Netflix
- Bob Haas (Ivory Coast 1964–1966), CEO of Levi
  Strauss & Co.

- George Packer (Togo 1982–1983), journalist, author of "The Assassins' Gate"
- Charles Murray (Thailand 1965–1968), political scientist, author of "The Bell Curve"
- Kinky Friedman (Malaysia 1967–1969), singer, Kinky Friedman and The Texas Jewboys
- Taylor Hackford (Bolivia 1968–1969), movie producer, "An Officer and a Gentleman"
- Alberto Ibargüen (Venezuela 1966–1968), CEO of the John S. and James L. Knight Foundation
- Lillian Carter (India 1966–1968), mother of President Jimmy Carter
- Michael McCaskey (Ethiopia 1965–1967), chairman of the board of the Chicago Bears.
- Karen DeWitt (Ethiopia 1966–1968), journalist and communications executive

The community of returned volunteers is bolstered by their family, friends, and colleagues, plus a large body of admirers and enthusiasts. I am an example of the latter. When Hershey was serving in Ethiopia, I was growing up in Peru, where my parents offered a home away from home to numerous Peace Corps volunteers. I was fascinated by their idealism, courage, and adventures—and I am fascinated still.

I hope you enjoy this book as much as I did.

Dr. John C. Green is director emeritus, Ray C. Bliss Institute of Applied Politics, The University of Akron

Foreword

RICHARD F. CELESTE

SOME PEACE CORPS volunteers (PCVs) thrive. Some just get by. A few just don't make it and come home early.

Bill Hershey exemplifies the PCV who thrives. His wonderfully told stories (and self-deprecating humor) convey the stuff of success in the Peace Corps. The volunteer lives in a (often remote) village. The volunteer eats like his neighbors, sleeps like his neighbors, even plays basketball like his neighbors.

A Peace Corps volunteer conveys American values in deeds more than works—modesty, hard work, curiosity, respect for others. And that volunteer learns as much as he or she teaches.

One story after another conveys how observant and respectful Bill was in his adopted home in Ethiopia. How patient he had to be when things didn't happen as fast as they might have at home in the United States or when words seemed to convey different meanings to the speaker and the listener.

One of the original goals of the Peace Corps Act was to bring back to the United States lessons learned and insights gained during service overseas. Bill Hershey has done that magnificently as a professional journalist, sharing delightful and sometimes uncomfortable stories of his life as a PCV in Ethiopia with folks in Akron and beyond.

I remember vividly my exchange with a Peace Corps volunteer in Senegal in 1979 when I was Peace Corps director. She had been working with the women of a village on the edge of the Sahara, creating a community garden. She was legally blind but had never mentioned that to the villagers when she would kneel on the ground to examine the garden.

As we were walking back to the village from the work site, I asked her what her service had meant to her. She said: "It has given me the gift of new eyes. I have come to see the women of my village in a way that I never could if I had stayed in Boston. And I see my country now in a fresh way—things that make me proud and things I would like to change."

She concluded: "And I now see myself in a new way. I have been able to do things that I never thought possible."

Bill Hershey has given us "the gift of new eyes."

Richard F. Celeste was Peace Corps director from 1979 to 1981, governor of Ohio from 1983 to 1991, United States ambassador to India from 1997 to 2001, and president of Colorado College from 2002 to 2011.

Foreword

BOB TAFT

WHEN THEY LEARN that I was a Peace Corps volunteer, my students at the University of Dayton often ask what it was like and if they should do the same. Now, I will be able to refer them to Bill Hershey's crisp and entertaining account of his service as a school teacher with the Peace Corps in Ethiopia in the late 1960s.

There are too few good books about the Peace Corps, which is unfortunate because the program that President Kennedy initiated six decades ago has been a remarkable success. As it was when I signed up in 1963, the Peace Corps remains a uniquely rewarding opportunity for Americans of all ages and talents and a source of expertise and training for peoples in low-income countries throughout the world.

By my senior year in college, I had visited a number of countries but had never lived overseas. It was a time of

idealism and hope for the future; new countries were emerg-
ing from the confines of colonialism. President Kennedy
challenged us—"ask not what your country can do for you,
but what you can do for your country." The Peace Corps
embodied that challenge and gave me the chance to learn and
test myself as a teacher in the faraway land of Tanzania.

Hershey is up front about the challenges Peace Corps volunteers face when they first arrive in a new country. He had to
take the plunge of learning a new language, eating new foods,
and comprehending local customs and beliefs. Like Bill, I had
to become accustomed to a loss of creature comforts and my
favorite foods and living in a community where the only other
American was a fellow Peace Corps teacher. Extending ourselves to adapt to new circumstances was a growth experience
for all of us who served.

One of the original goals of the Peace Corps was to promote a better understanding of other peoples on the part of
Americans. My experiences helped me appreciate the amazing hospitality and generosity of Tanzanians, who possessed
little in the way of worldly possessions. One of my students,
Salvus Shiponya, invited me to come home with him during
a school break. When I arrived at the small compound of huts
with thatched roofs where he lived, far out in the countryside,
his family insisted I sleep in their only bed. They heated water
on a woodburning fire for me to bathe and, as I departed,
presented me with a live chicken to carry home on my bicycle.
This was an experience I will never forget. Bill Hershey shares
stories of similar acts of common humanity by his Ethiopian
friends and associates.

The Peace Corps also promotes a better understanding of Americans on the part of peoples in host countries. In particular, volunteers present a view of our country very different from and more authentic than that portrayed in movies and mass media. A cross section of American volunteers with varying backgrounds, beliefs, and abilities creates close personal relationships with people in host countries, giving rise to friendships and new perceptions about our country. Bill Hershey tells the story of how he built strong connections with his students, fellow teachers and local Ethiopians, enabling him to weather cultural misunderstandings and anti-American attitudes on the part of some Ethiopians.

A principal purpose of the Peace Corps has been to meet the need for more well-trained people across the developing world in fields such as education, health, agriculture, environmental protection and youth development. Bill and I served this purpose in similar ways as teachers. We helped our middle school students master their coursework so they would have a chance to excel on a national exam that determined admission into high school.

From a political viewpoint, "Taking the Plunge into Ethiopia" is a more interesting book than I might have written about my time as a Peace Corps volunteer. Tanganyika did merge with Zanzibar and became Tanzania during my tour of duty. However, unlike Ethiopia, Tanzania in the 1960s had stable one-party rule under President Julius Nyerere, a leader in its independence movement. By contrast, during Bill's tour in Ethiopia, the country was starting to experience political turmoil, a prelude to its transition from aging Emperor Haile

Selassie, a U.S. ally, to a Marxist military government aligned
with the Soviet Union and Cuba. As the sole American in the
community where he served, Bill was forced to navigate these
tensions. He does a masterful job of describing the tense inci-
dents he faced and how he, unlike some other volunteers in
the country, was able to prevail and complete his mission of
educating the next generation of Ethiopians.

Hershey recalls how he would engage in debates with
Ethiopian university students performing a year of national
service at his school. This brings to mind one of the main
benefits of Peace Corps service for American volunteers:
seeing how people in host countries eke out a living in places
without electricity or running water or paved roads can lead
to a greater appreciation for the standard of living we have in
the United States. It also highlights the political freedoms we
enjoy, which are often not prevalent in so many countries. Just
the challenge of explaining and often defending the U.S. to
people in the host country gave me a deeper understanding
of our own system of government and of some of the com-
parative advantages of life in the U.S.

Bill includes an account of how he helped Abraham, one
of his former students, immigrate to the U.S., graduate from
college and start a new chapter of his life here. This story
illustrates the kind of constructive impact that returned
Peace Corps volunteers can have on the U.S. More than
240,000 volunteers who served in 142 different countries have
returned since 1961. They bring back invaluable knowledge
and understanding of other cultures and nationalities to
enrich and inform communities across the U.S. This impact

should be counted as one of the important benefits of the Peace Corps.

The Peace Corps is a government initiative that has stood the test of time and received strong bipartisan support from our elected officials throughout its history. In this fascinating and informative account of his adventures in Ethiopia, Bill Hershey helps us understand why the Peace Corps lives on today and how it brings people together to create new opportunities and build more vibrant communities across the world.

Bob Taft was a Peace Corps volunteer in East Africa. The country he served in was called Tanganyika when he started in 1963 and was renamed Tanzania by the time his service ended in 1965. He was governor of Ohio from 1999 to 2007 and secretary of state of Ohio from 1991 to 1999. Since 2007 he has been a distinguished research associate at the University of Dayton.

Introduction

WILLIAM HERSHEY

IT'S BEEN 55 years since I arrived in Dabat, Ethiopia, the small town where I spent two years teaching seventh- and eighth-grade English as a Peace Corps volunteer.

I can still see the dusty, unpaved road splitting the town and smell the buses and trucks belching diesel fumes as they passed through. The whitewashed houses of wood and mud with their tin roofs still live in my memory.

Most of all, I remember the students, teachers and townspeople who welcomed me, the only American in town, into their lives.

The Peace Corps, which celebrated its 60th anniversary in 2021, still earns bipartisan support, a rarity in our increasingly polarized politics. Democratic president John F. Kennedy founded the Peace Corps, and his brother-in-law Sargent Shriver was the first director. The longest serving director, however, was Loret Miller Ruppe, who ran the agency from 1981–1989 under Republican Ronald Reagan.

More than 240,000 volunteers have served in more than 140 countries. Each has his or her own story about teaching school, eradicating disease, developing a local economy or providing whatever service the host country desired.

The magazine articles and newspaper columns in this book span 41 years, reflecting the lasting influence of the Peace Corps on my life and how I see the world. As a newspaper reporter, I spent decades covering local, state and national governments and reporting on political campaigns.

Peace Corps memories kept poking through, however. The three magazine articles, all written while I was still working, let me reflect on the cross-cultural challenge of getting a school outhouse cleaned, the global fellowship of a dirt court basketball game and the bravery of refugees cast adrift by war.

After retiring in 2012, I used the shorter newspaper columns to examine divisive issues such as America's role in the world, immigration, and religious conflict through the lens of my Peace Corps experience.

That experience was a happy accident. It gave me the chance to live in one of the world's oldest civilizations, with a history dating back to the 10th century BCE. I got to learn Amharic, the official Ethiopian language. Ethiopian food—*wat,* a spicy stew made with different materials (eggs, lentils, potatoes, vegetables, sheep, chicken, or beef) and *injera,* a pancake-like bread—became my everyday diet. I met my future wife Marcia, a volunteer in a nearby town. We've been married 52 years.

Until finishing up a one-year graduate school program in 1968, I had not considered the Peace Corps. I was offered several jobs as a newspaper reporter upon graduation and at first decided to accept one. The Vietnam War was raging, however, and young men my age, 23, were likely to be drafted. I wanted to avoid that.

A graduate school friend began talking to me about the Peace Corps. He had served in the Ivory Coast in West Africa and spoke fondly of his experiences.

Peace Corps service would provide a draft deferment.

There was a touch of idealism in my decision to apply. At Albion College, the liberal arts school in Michigan that I graduated from, there were regular calls for social justice, international understanding and using America's wealth to improve the lives of the poor, at home and abroad.

The most plainspoken admonition came from Dr. Joseph Washington, dean of the chapel: stop talking and start doing.

So, I applied.

I emphasized my knowledge of Spanish. I had studied the language for six years, and our family had hosted a student from El Salvador when I was in high school. Surely the Peace Corps would find an assignment in Central or South America.

When I was accepted to teach English in Ethiopia, I needed a map to locate the country on Africa's eastern horn. I had heard of Emperor Haile Selassie but knew nothing else about Ethiopia.

That changed in an intense training program that began in June and didn't end until September just before school started. I trained first at a summer camp in Maine and then in Nazret in southern Ethiopia. We got a start at learning Amharic, Ethiopian history and culture and teaching methods.

We also got a hint of the political unrest bubbling up in Ethiopia. The volunteers knew that in 1968 America was tearing itself apart with the assassinations of Martin Luther King, Jr. and Robert Kennedy, angry protests against the Vietnam War, and a civil rights movement marked by peaceful demonstrations and urban rioting.

What many of us didn't know was that Ethiopia was undergoing its own political eruptions that would result in the overthrow of Haile Selassie in 1974. The emperor, crowned in 1930, had earned an international reputation as a brave leader after pleading with the League of Nations in 1935 for help against an invasion by Italy that used chemical warfare and mustard gas. The League did nothing, and the emperor went into exile in England for five years before returning in triumph in 1941 when the country was liberated. He began efforts to modernize the country and educate more of its citizens.

Still, a wide gap existed between the rural poverty in much of the country and the luxurious lifestyle enjoyed by the emperor and a small elite.

Some of our Ethiopian trainers let us know that they resented the United States for supporting Haile Selassie and didn't want us in their country.

That didn't stop us from getting our assignments and reporting for our teaching duties.

Originally, another male volunteer and I were assigned to a school with grades one through eight in Dabat (pronounced *DAH-baht*), a small town in northern Ethiopia with no running water or electricity and an elevation of about 8,500 feet. Dabat's population in 2022 was estimated at 11,544 by the World Population Review. I don't know the 1968 population but am sure it was smaller.

We arrived in Gondar, the region's provincial capital, and took a get-acquainted trip to Dabat before school started. Unfortunately, both of us got sick after an evening of Ethiopian hospitality featuring too much to eat and drink.

The other volunteer decided to stay in Gondar, leaving me as the only volunteer in Dabat. I had to quickly adapt to the culture. I had to plunge or perish.

I took the plunge and had plenty of help.

The police captain, whose name I can't recall, rented me the new house he had just built for himself for my first year. The second year I moved in with Shumbeza, a fellow teacher.

Demoz, the school director, made me feel like I belonged, both in faculty meetings and out-of-school get-togethers.

It may be a cliché, but sports really is an international language. The Ethiopian teachers and I found common ground on the dirt basketball and volleyball courts.

I wasn't the only volunteer on the faculty. Ethiopian university students were required to spend a year teaching at schools throughout the country. There was friction between Peace Corps teachers and these university students in some places. Some were anti-American Marxists who ridiculed the Peace Corps volunteers and bad-mouthed them to their classes.

In the neighboring town of Debarek, where my future wife Marcia and her housemate Gwen taught, two university students caused trouble in their second year. They tried to turn the students against them but failed. Marcia and Gwen by then had earned a reservoir of goodwill with the other teachers and students.

Two volunteers in another town were brutally beaten.

I was lucky. Bahru and Girma, the two university service teachers my first year in Dabat, became friends. One of my favorite keepsakes is a photo of the three of us visiting the Blue Nile Falls near Lake Tana in northern Ethiopia. I wasn't as close to the university students the second year, but we got along.

Outside the school, Beyene, a prosperous local merchant, used one of his trucks to transport a stove and other belongings to Dabat. He wouldn't take any money because I was the teacher of his children.

Tefela, the shopkeeper from Yemen, cashed my checks and enjoyed our conversations in English and Amharic.

Aba Mekibb, the government clerk, liked it when I joined him at a local watering hole for *tella,* homemade Ethiopian beer.

Mamit, the owner of Dabat's top bar-hotel-restaurant, sold me takeout Ethiopian food most of my first year and provided delicious injera and wat when out-of-town Peace Corps bigshots visited. She even forgave me for unintentionally insulting her when I addressed her with a pronoun not showing the proper respect. She was pleased that on a trip to Addis Ababa, the Ethiopian capital, I brought back cassettes of Ethiopian music to provide battery-powered entertainment for her customers.

One of Mamit's barmaids saved me from a beating one night when I was walking home alone and was confronted by a mob of students displeased with my teaching methods and their grades. She shooed them away.

My most important connection, however, was with the students. Many were poor and came to school barefoot, with pencils about the length of a finger. They were hungry to learn, and I tried to feed them.

Some Peace Corps volunteers dismissed teaching English as irrelevant in an underdeveloped, mostly rural country. I disagreed.

All classes except Amharic were taught in English starting with the seventh grade. The English my students learned in Dabat was a tool that they needed to get ahead.

I wanted to get them speaking English, not just learning from a book. I had gone to school in Flint, Michigan, now a poster city for the decline of American manufacturing. Back then Flint was a boomtown with outstanding schools.

My high school Spanish teacher, Jerald Graves, immersed us in Spanish, much as our Peace Corps trainers had immersed us in Amharic. Señor Graves used a scripted dialog to get us talking with each other. I used my English version of his dialog to open most classes. The students got used to saying, "good morning" and asking each other "how are you?" and "who is that?" It took a little getting used to, especially for the girls who were taught to be deferential, but most students embraced it.

In addition to teaching English, I taught math for one year and also taught first-grade games for a short time.

Besides teaching, I supported two students each year by having them live with me. Some Ethiopian teachers also sponsored poor students.

My Peace Corps service became a family affair. I am an only child, and my mom Josephine and my dad Clark back in Flint were eager to keep up with what was going on. We exchanged letters and taped messages. My mother's church group provided financial support for a poor student.

My dad, then 60, was legally blind and retired from General Motors. He decided to visit Ethiopia. My mom wanted to come, but her asthma prevented this. In Dabat we butchered a sheep in dad's honor for a feast. He adjusted well to the outhouse with the on-the-ground slit.

We toured the country by car, airplane, and cart and horse. I didn't take him on the buses where standing room only and three passengers to a seat was common.

Even by plane, he got a taste of Ethiopian travel. At one stop he said something like, "Bill, I think a sheep just came aboard." He was right.

Some volunteers returned home early in 1970 because their schools were closed due to student unrest. I made it to the end of the school year in Dabat and planned to return to Ethiopia for a third year after home leave. On the trip to the United States, however, I contracted malaria, which was diagnosed after I got to Flint.

I recovered and stayed in the United States. Marcia and I got married, and we returned to Ethiopia in 1973 to work as Peace Corps trainers. Haile Selassie was deposed about a year after we got home. We haven't been back to Ethiopia, but the Peace Corps experience still is a big part of our lives.

The Outhouse Rebellion*

IT WAS AN enchanting night. There were no streetlights, no neon signs flashing ads for "hamburgs," cut-rate mufflers and eternal life. The only brightness came from the moon and the stars, blinking through a hazeless sky.

It was hushed beauty, interrupted only by the occasional cry of a hyena.

But suddenly the poetic silence was broken. Rocks came crashing down on the tin roof at the house of the only American in town. Then the rustle of footsteps faded away into the no longer beautiful darkness.

A short time later there was another assault on the mud and stone house, another cascade of rocks bouncing off the tin roof.

The rock attacks were threats. Earlier the same day, students armed with clubs and rocks had roamed the town's only

* © William Hershey, Akron Beacon Journal, Beacon Magazine, USA Today Network, April 19, 1981.

street. They'd attacked a Land Rover passing through, carrying two Americans and two English graduate students.

The four escaped serious injury, but the glass in two of the
Land Rover's windows was shattered.

All that didn't happen in El Salvador, Iran, or some other
recent site of anti-American activity. It took place in Ethiopia
in 1970.

Often called the "Hidden Empire," Ethiopia in 1981 is
under the influence of Russian and Cuban Communists—so
it will probably be "hidden" from most Americans for at least
the near future.

But in the late 1960s and early '70s the same sort of turmoil that has recently rocked Iran and El Salvador was turning things upside down in Ethiopia.

The house I shared with an Ethiopian teacher withstood
the barrage of rocks, but the experience remains in my memory's active file. I was one of several hundred Peace Corps
volunteers stationed in Ethiopia as teachers. We'd come for
various reasons—to dodge the draft and avoid Vietnam, to
see the world and—in a few cases—to save it with liberal
doses of American idealism.

Most of us came with little idea of what Ethiopia was like
and little appreciation of its rich, ancient culture. I knew the
country was in Africa, but I had to check a map to find out
just where. We left the country with a sobering view of the
revolution that would soon topple His Imperial Majesty Haile
Selassie I, Conquering Lion of the Tribe of Judah, King of
Kings and Elect of God from his imperial throne—and that
would eventually install a Marxist military government
served by Russian advisers and Cuban soldiers.

There were no network television crews to send the beginning of the Ethiopian uprising back to Main Street, U.S.A. But I can still conjure mental pictures of the *shinte bete* imbroglio, the name I gave to our little town's slice of the revolution to come.

Roughly translated, the phrase means a confusing disagreement about an outhouse. (The latter is pronounced *SHIN-tah-bait*.) But not all the volunteers who got in the way of the Ethiopian revolution felt like giving their experiences funny names.

One volunteer was on a plane hijacked to the Sudan by a group of Ethiopian university students. Among the hijackers was a student I'd known; I'd incorrectly sized him up as someone who talked a good revolution, but probably wouldn't try to make one.

The hijacked volunteer was safely returned to Ethiopia—but, like many of the Americans in my Peace Corps group, he left the country before his two full years of service were up.

Two other volunteers left early after getting beaten up in the town where they were teaching.

The rebellion, then, wasn't an isolated incident. It was part of a course of events that started before my arrival and continued until Haile Selassie's downfall.

Fortunately for me, Dabat, the town where I spent two years, was about as unlikely a place for revolution as existed in Ethiopia. There was no running water, no electricity, and a single dirt road passed through town.

Dabat is in northern Ethiopia. It's a section of the country from which kings had come centuries before, but then generally ignored by the Selassie regime, student rebels and everybody else.

But there were shortwave radios in Dabat, bringing to the elementary and junior high students news of what was happening in Addis Ababa, the nation's capital. Most often the news of unrest at Haile Selassie University came from the BBC, the Voice of America or Radio Moscow.

Radio Ethiopia had little to say about the clashes between university students and government troops that occasionally resulted in dead students, and often resulted in shutting down the college.

The students in Dabat were beginning to understand the reasons for the clashes. They knew the emperor lived in splendor and traveled around the world, hailed as Africa's greatest statesman. Radio Ethiopia and their textbooks told them that much.

Their textbooks didn't tell them what they already knew though, that in their town and the surrounding countryside people had little to eat and no reason to think conditions would improve for their children.

From the university students doing national service they would hear details of the vast differences separating a small elite in Addis Ababa and a few other cities from the rest of the country's people.

Such lessons weren't part of the regular course of study. They were taught covertly, often in informal chats with students not suspected of being informers. Bahru, a university service teacher my first year, made one such presentation to a whole class—but only after making sure there were no observers from town listening in.

As students gained an awareness of their nation's problems, it wasn't surprising that anti-Americanism grew. After all, the United States was the great friend of Haile Selassie. Even Radio Ethiopia said that.

And many of the Peace Corps volunteers displayed a sort of clumsiness in adjusting to the local culture. In Ethiopia, roles were rigidly defined. Adults ate first. The children ate what was left. Old people were respected, not laughed at or put in nursing homes.

Americans, with their naïve ideas about treating everybody alike, were in for a rude awakening if they didn't at least keep quiet.

Even when they were successful at blending in, the volunteers were the most visible evidence of what became an increasingly unwelcome American presence.

"*Ferenji* (foreigner) go home!" became the students' national rallying cry. I survived the first year in Dabat with relatively few taunts and no real threats. The university students in Dabat weren't as militant as some of their colleagues in other cities. After a few beers or a rowdy weekend together in the provincial capital, they would even concede that I might not be a CIA agent.

Our disputes in Dabat were verbal. We would argue heatedly, but usually go home to sleep, not to find rocks or clubs.

It helped, too, that there were no other Americans in town. In larger cities, the volunteers frequently lived apart from the Ethiopians. They'd come 8,000 miles to experience life in another culture—and ended up living in compounds cut off from the rest of the country. They prided themselves on cooks who could prepare French fries, tuna fish casseroles and peanut butter cookies. Their unwillingness to eat Ethiopian food, speak the language and socialize with their hosts made them easy marks for the propagandizing of student revolutionaries.

Despite my fondness for Ethiopian food and a passing familiarity with Amharic, the rebellion would prove that I couldn't cope with the culture as well as I thought.

The outhouse rebellion had its roots in a routine inspection of the school at the end of my first year by the Ethiopian provincial education minister. He had complained to the school director that the shinte betes were filthy, which they were. No one cleaned them regularly.

In our part of Ethiopia, manual labor was frowned upon. Cleaning toilets was for servants and the school didn't have any—unless you counted the watchman, whose job description didn't include latrine duty.

When the next year started, my roommate and I were put in charge of the Welfare Club. That meant we collected money for tea for the teachers to drink during their breaks, with any left over going to worthwhile projects such as helping students.

We made, it turned out, a near-fatal mistake. My roommate, who came from a part of Ethiopia where manual labor wasn't frowned upon, was nearly as much a foreigner in the community as I was. He was derisively called a "clothes seller," a description of the work that occupied many people in his part of the country.

At any rate, we decided to buy some brooms and bleach. We gave the students the tools to clean the shinte betes, which consisted of holes made in concrete foundations, surrounded by brick and concrete walls.

Each week a different homeroom was to clean the shinte betes, a plan that worked fine—for about two weeks.

The students in my eighth-grade homeroom and the other eighth-grade homeroom did their duties, albeit not happily. But other students wanted no part of the job, and their teachers didn't push them.

Eventually, I told my students to forget it. Shine bete neglect took over once again. The plot thickened when the school director decided the outhouses should be cleaned. At that time, the director already was feeling the heat from students and townspeople who suspected him of pocketing money from the sale of grass in the school compound. (The "grass" was of the regular variety, to be sold for animal feed.) This time I wasn't in charge of shinte bete cleaning; the task had fallen to Demissie, who was the school health officer.

He had little appreciation for the growing political awareness of the students. I don't know how he informed students they would be shinte bete cleaners again, but they didn't like his presentation.

The brooms and bleach, meanwhile, had disappeared—so the director told the students to sweep the outhouses with leaves. That was the method used to clean out most of the classrooms.

The Welfare Club came to the rescue with more brooms and bleach, but the students weren't satisfied. The shinte betes had become a symbol of resistance to the director.

"Our parents didn't send us to school to clean the shinte betes," a student told me. "They sent us to school to learn."

During the battle of wills, I became a shinte bete hawk. I saw nothing wrong with the cleaning assignment even if it violated their cultural tradition and it put me on the side of the suspect school director.

We approached a standoff. The students wouldn't clean the outhouses. The director wouldn't let them in their classes.

One afternoon, leaders of one student faction started pulling students not involved in the dispute out of their classes. The school compound turned into a battleground. Rocks flew. Students used clubs to clobber other students who didn't want to come out of class and protest.

Town police were called in. A day later, army troops from the provincial capital showed up.

A student who lived with me advised me to stay home. Much of the blame for the shinte bete cleaning was being placed on me and my foreign ideas. My ferenji notions had put the director up to the whole thing, some students charged.

I went home—and that was the night that rocks descended on my roof. Several Ethiopians and I grouped for a counterattack. We stalked through the town and nearby countryside looking for the rock throwers.

Fortunately, we found none. Two of the Ethiopians had handguns, and a third carried a rifle. Not wanting to overstay my welcome, I prepared to leave Ethiopia. "I'll be home for Easter," became my rallying cry.

It didn't turn out that way. The Dabat rebellion passed more quickly than uprisings in the rest of the country. Only my ego was damaged. In a few days the parents, students and the school director negotiated a fragile truce that saw the students return to class.

About 100 students showed up at my house to ask me to stay. The assistant to the district governor even made a plea.

I'd like to think the sudden show of fondness paid tribute to my wizardry of cross-cultural understanding—but it had more to do with the students' desire to pass the eighth-grade national examinations that were needed to qualify for high school.

So I stayed. The shinte betes got dirty again, and nobody said much. The school year ended, and the Ethiopian teachers presented me with a set of national clothes—white knickers, a white blouse and a shawl.

For me, the experiences of good times and hospitality from the people of an ancient culture had outweighed the bad.

When my wife and I had the chance to return to Ethiopia three years later as Peace Corps trainers, we willingly made the trip—with our two-year-old daughter.

Our second coming was generally uneventful, but our timing was good. We returned to the United States in the fall of 1973. Less than a year later, Haile Selassie was overthrown. Anti-Americanism became not just a student rallying cry, but the policy of the new Ethiopian military government.

My Brief But Dismal Career on the Ethiopian Basketball Circuit*

IT'S BEEN HISTORY for several weeks that Wes Unseld erased Marvin Webster, and the Washington Bullets finally quit choking and ended up as the 1978 champions of the National Basketball Association.

But forgive me if I don't get up for Unseld, Elvin "The Big E" Hayes and the other Bullets—or down with the Seattle Supersonics and their failed attempt to become the Amazing Mets of the Great Northwest.

You see, basketball in the NBA is merely a simple layup when you've tasted international competition on the rooftop of Africa under the protecting pistol of an Ethiopian police captain. The Doctor may have the slam dunk, but it was a certain "Mr. Bill" who brought the standing jump shot to Dabat, Ethiopia, which before his arrival was unknown as a cradle of basketball greatness.

---

* © William Hershey, Akron Beacon Journal, Beacon Magazine, USA Today Network, July 2, 1978.

If you haven't noticed, this is an immodest tale, somehow ignored by the international sporting press but still demanding to be told—nearly a decade after this reporter ended his one-game international career as Dabat's all-time leading American scorer. Let us begin.

Like all good basketball stories, this one has a humble beginning. No Indiana farm—with or without a wire hoop on the barn—or rundown urban tenement full of waiting-to-be-discovered hoop phenoms can compare with Dabat for humbleness. When I arrived there as a Peace Corps teacher in 1968, there was no running water nor electricity, about three telephones and a local government housed in what appeared to be the bombed-out remains of a building.

There also was a school—block buildings with tin roofs for the seventh and eighth graders and buildings made of dried mud for their elementary classmates. Close by the mud classrooms was the Ethiopian version of James Naismith's invention. Square backboards with wire rims were mounted on tree trunks at each end of a dirt rectangle. It wasn't Madison Square Garden.

The basketball court had been carved out by Ethiopian teachers with help from a previous Peace Corps volunteer.

Dabat's modest physical and technological appointments were well suited to my previously undistinguished athletic career. I was one of the few aspirants to have been trimmed from the Flint, Michigan Central junior varsity football squad. Faster and quicker basketball prospects had been passing me by since the seventh grade. It had been an athletic career dogged continually by the description "fat but slow" and "short but clumsy."

But the air was thin in Dabat—as it will be at elevations of 8,000 feet—and visions of athletic mediocrity, if not outright greatness, began dribbling in my head during increasingly frequent after-school basketball games with students and faculty. Never mind that I had a 23-year (my age at the time) head start over my new playmates. They cheered at my barely jumping jump shot and flinched at my clumsy but uncompromising defense.

We bounced our way through October and November—months of pleasant weather in the rugged Ethiopian central highlands—but it became obvious we wanted a test. The thrill of intramural victory no longer was enough. Several Ethiopian teachers had learned basketball at teacher-training institutes—after playing two or three years, they were about my equal—and they, along with the school director, decided we would challenge the nearby town of Azezo to a match.

The challenge would give us the home court advantage, and the two schools would meet in early December for an afternoon of basketball and volleyball, a game the Ethiopians play much more physically than most Americans.

The Ethiopian "invitation"—as our match was called—requires a brief explanation. It's a throwback to the days in early America when the good old boys from one town crowded into their good old cars, traveled to the next town for an afternoon of basketball and stayed around to eat and drink with their rivals.

It was no different in Dabat—except the visitors arrived in wheezing buses, not their good old cars. When game day arrived, the dirt rectangle was surrounded by a crowd of Ethiopians in various forms of dress. Old men with white blankets—a form of national dress—stood shoulder to shoulder with officers from the local army camp and teachers dressed in "woolens," wool suits that were an uncomfortable status symbol in a climate where the sun shone almost continually.

There were the obligatory pregame festivities. Soul handshakes had not made their way to the highlands, but the Ethiopians have their own greeting, dating back centuries. Teachers greeted teachers with firm hugs and kisses to each cheek. It may not have been American macho, but it was their country, not mine.

We entered the court, one by one. It was definitely the biggest home—or away—crowd I ever had played before. The previous highlight of my basketball career had been a state tournament for church teams. I was the "sixth man" on a team that lost two straight games before a crowd that must have numbered at least 15 parents. There were several hundred Ethiopians around for this big one.

So, we started. Ragged but rough, the game moved through the first half in what sportswriters might describe as a cliffhanger. One or two baskets separated the teams for most of the half. My assignment was to contain *Ato* (Mr.) Yohannes, Azezo's backcourt leader. I contained him properly the first time by cleanly knocking the ball from his hand as he moved in for what looked to be an uncontested layup. The crowd loved it.

Ato Yohannes didn't, however, and the ground was laid for what nearly became Dabat's "international incident." On my second effort at containment, I knocked not only the ball but a good part of Ato Yohannes's arm.

"Why don't you slow down?" he asked, not pleasantly. Encouraged by the crowd, I made an equally unpleasant reply. Ato Yohannes was ready to flatten me. His teammates were bigger than mine, so it looked like he might get the job done. Retreat seemed in order, but the Dabat captain thought this was a hot dog move and told me to return. I did, but to no avail. The final score is a distant memory, but Azezo finished with more points than Dabat.

We did win the ensuing volleyball match—with no help from me—and saved face for the postgame banquet. We washed down our afternoon of fellowship with plenty of Ethiopian beer and finished off the better part of a freshly roasted sheep. There was much talk of brotherhood and the ropes of friendship stretching from Dabat to Azezo.

It wasn't until the visitors departed that I learned I had little to fear during my exchange with Yohannes. "He had a bad conduct," one of my students informed me. (That doesn't translate too well, but it's something like a very bad attitude.)

The student said I should have flattened Yohannes. There was nothing to fear, he added: The police captain, ever alert to protecting his guest, had his hand on his pistol—ready to fire should there be any real danger to the American presence.

There are "enforcers" in the NBA, of course, but the pistols usually are left at the door.

My international playing days no doubt are behind me. It's been all downhill since that sunny afternoon. All that's left is banging around the small gym at Akron's downtown YMCA on days when there is at least one other player as untalented as this one.

There are occasional jeers at a missed shot and unfriendly protests from some former high school hotshot when a slow-moving hand misses the ball and cracks the wrist. But what do they know? They can dunk, but they've never played in Dabat.

My Plunge into Ethiopia[*]

J. CHRISTOPHER STEVENS, the American ambassador to Libya killed on September 11, 2012, in an attack on a consulate in Benghazi, went to Morocco as a Peace Corps volunteer in 1983.

From all accounts of Stevens's inspiring life and tragic death, the two years he spent teaching English as a volunteer was a prelude to the rest of his life. He became, a New York Times' headline said, "a U.S. envoy who plunged into Arab life."

Stevens's determination to get out of the embassy and into the Arab street made him different than some ambassadors. His approach, however, described the key to success for the more than 210,000 Peace Corps volunteers who have served in 139 countries from 1961–2012.

Stevens's story awakened memories of the two years I spent teaching English as a volunteer in Dabat, Ethiopia, from 1968 to 1970.

---

* © William Hershey, Akron Beacon Journal, USA Today Network, September 21, 2012.

As the only American in the small town of about 1,000 residents, it was plunge or perish.

I plunged.

Stevens was fluent in Arabic. I was adequate in Amharic, the Ethiopian language, good enough to be understood but not good enough to avoid unintentional insults.

The plunge made that OK.

Injera and wat became the staple of my diet. *Tella* and *tej*—homemade Ethiopian beer and wine—were my beverages of choice.

Tefela, the shopkeeper, Mamit, the bar owner, Beyene, the landlord and Mekebebe, the government clerk, forgave my shortcomings because I did my best to understand life in one of the world's oldest countries with a history tracing back to pre-biblical times.

The Ethiopian teachers were my friends. One, Shumbeza, was my roommate. We ate together, hit the bars together and played basketball and volleyball on our school's dirt courts.

The students were hungry for their lessons and sometimes desperately clever. One poor but very bright boy wrote his own tests left-handed and then did a right-handed version for a more affluent—by Ethiopian standards—girl who paid him.

My primary responsibility was seventh- and eighth-grade English, but I also taught first-grade games.

Starting in the seventh grade, all classes were taught in English. The English they learned was a tool they could use to build better lives for themselves.

The students also delighted in our dramatic presentation of "United Nations Day," role-playing with thespian zeal.

The world then, as now, could be dangerous and unwelcoming for Americans. In Ethiopia, Marxist college students, not Islamic radicals, led the anti-American chorus. All Ethiopian college students were required to do a year of service as teachers in schools across the country. This caused problems for some Peace Corps volunteers. Some of the university service teachers did their best to turn their students against America.

Two volunteers I knew were beaten badly by an angry student mob.

In Dabat, however, Bahru and Girma, university service teachers, became good friends.

Sadly, nothing like the Arab Spring that Ambassador Stevens helped achieve followed my tour in Ethiopia. Instead, a military junta deposed Emperor Haile Selassie in 1974 and established a ruthless socialist regime that rebels finally ousted in 1991.

Conditions have improved, but the agriculture-based economy still produces per capita income among the lowest in the world.

I have not been back to Ethiopia since working in a volunteer training program in 1973. I have remained in touch with teachers and students, however. One student, Abraham, was resettled in the United States with the help of Akron's First Presbyterian Church after he became a refugee during fighting against the socialist government.

While Stevens's life ended tragically, Abraham applauded how the ambassador tried to help the Libyan people.

"It smoothed out the road to what he wanted to accomplish," Abraham said.

My 1968 in Ethiopia[*]

AMERICANS ARE OBSESSED with 50-year commemorations, and 1968 marks an important one for historically significant and solemn reasons.

It is also a 50th year commemoration personally, for reasons directly related to those that made 1968 stand out for the nation.

The Vietnam War that year was becoming an uneasy presence in the national consciousness.

The reality of the war gained a sharper and frightening focus in January when North Vietnamese and Vietcong troops launched the Tet offensive against American and South Vietnamese forces.

The Americans and South Vietnamese ultimately prevailed, but it was a propaganda victory for the enemy, sending a message that they were capable of sustained and full-scale warfare.

---

[*] © William Hershey, Akron Beacon Journal, USA Today Network, February 25, 2018.

Three months later, on April 4, the nation was shocked by the assassination in Memphis, Tennessee, of the Rev. Martin Luther King, Jr., who had become the face of the long-overdue national civil rights crusade.

Just two months later on June 5, the country was shocked again, this time by the assassination of U.S. Senator Robert Kennedy, fresh from his victory in the California Democratic presidential primary.

Few of us were passive bystanders to these cataclysmic developments. I was finishing graduate school and trying to decide what to do with the rest of my life. It wasn't a decision that I could make on my own.

There were more than 500,000 American troops in Vietnam, and I knew that I was likely to be drafted when my student deferment expired, a possibility I didn't welcome.

At the same time, the two assassinations had left many of us disillusioned. It seemed like a good time to leave the country.

A graduate school friend mentioned the Peace Corps, which I had not considered. This, by the way, is Peace Corps Week, commemorating its start on March 1, 1961. Joining would defer the draft for two more years but not substitute for military service ultimately.

A combination of self-interest—to avoid the draft—and an admonition from a college chaplain convinced me to apply. The chaplain was tired of young people protesting national and global problems but doing nothing to solve them. "Do something," he said.

The government approved sending me halfway around the world to Ethiopia, an East African nation where Amharic, an ancient language with a complicated alphabet, was the official language.

In retrospect, I was lucky in 1968 to land in Dabat, a small Ethiopian town where I was the only American and taught English as a second language to junior high school students.

I learned important lessons. First, humility. It was difficult to forget how fortunate Americans were as I taught barefoot students, some clad in tattered shorts and shirts, using pencil stubs no longer than my thumb. Their hunger for learning still amazes me.

My hometown, Flint, Michigan, had a diverse population, but white people—mostly men—were the majority and almost always in charge.

Not in Ethiopia, a country occupied only briefly by the Italians during World War II.

In Dabat, I was in the racial minority for the first time in my life.

The teachers and townspeople embraced my willingness to fit in by eating Ethiopian food and speaking fractured Amharic, but there was no special treatment from the school's Ethiopian headmaster.

I forget the particular offense, but he once assigned me to teach first-grade games to students with no English. The students and I figured it out together and came up with a fast-paced Amharic version of "Duck, Duck, Goose."

While the benefits to me were clear, it is harder to judge how much difference Peace Corps volunteers made in Ethiopia.

We didn't help usher in representative democracy.

Ethiopia was a feudal society ruled by Emperor Haile Selassie when we arrived. The emperor was deposed in 1974 and replaced by a military government called the Derg, which established a reign of terror resulting in mass killings.

The Derg was overthrown in 1991, but the government in 2018 is dominated by one small ethnic group.

The benefits we provided, however, were personal. All classes were taught in English starting with the seventh grade. The English I taught equipped my students to further their educations and find jobs that improved their lives.

I had planned to return to Ethiopia for a third year, but during home leave I became seriously ill. After visits to more than three hospitals, the doctors correctly diagnosed me with malaria.

The draft board caught up with me as I recovered.

My doctor told me, however, that the malaria made me medically ineligible for the draft. He was right.

Finally, the Doctors Arrived at Malaria[*]

THE FRIGHTENING OUTBREAK of Ebola in West Africa that has already claimed more than 4,000 lives is a deadly reminder of priceless blessings that Americans too often take for granted:

A first-rate public health system and near immunity from diseases such as Ebola that still spread medical terror through less developed regions of the world.

Americans who have traveled or lived abroad probably have more appreciation for this than others. Yet, our system is not infallible.

The recent reported failure of a Dallas hospital to initially recognize Ebola in a patient and to send him home with antibiotics, only to later admit him was a haunting reminder of my own experience with well-intentioned, but not always

* © William Hershey, Akron Beacon Journal, USA Today Network, October 10, 2014.

perfect, American medicine more than 40 years ago while a
Peace Corps volunteer in Ethiopia in East Africa.

The patient in Dallas, identified as Thomas Eric Duncan,
died on Wednesday.

My experience involved malaria, more common than
Ebola and not contagious, but deadly if not treated. A bite
from an infected female mosquito introduces the parasites
causing malaria into the patient's blood. In 2012, according
to the World Health Organization, there were about 207 million malaria cases worldwide and an estimated 627,000
deaths—nearly as many deaths as there are people in the
cities of Cleveland and Cincinnati. Nearly 3.4 billion people—
half of the world's population—are at risk of malaria, according to the organization.

The Bill and Melinda Gates Foundation has put a global
spotlight on this mosquito-transmitted disease by making the
reduction and ultimate elimination of malaria a top priority.

Malaria was not a common problem in Dabat, the small
Ethiopian town where I taught school from 1968–1970. Dabat
was located more than a mile—8,563 feet—above sea level,
hardly mosquito territory.

The Peace Corps, however, advised all volunteers to take
weekly doses of malaria-prevention medicine. While some of
us were not stationed in malaria areas, we traveled from time
to time to areas where malaria was prevalent.

For two years, I took my medicine as I was told, Dabat's
elevation notwithstanding.

I had volunteered for a third year, however, and qualified
for a leave of several weeks in the summer of 1970 to travel
home to Michigan. That's when the problem occurred.

With a good Peace Corps friend, I celebrated my way back to the U.S., traveling across Africa with tourist stops in the Ivory Coast, Ghana, Nigeria and Liberia.

Unlike Dabat, many areas we visited were not more than a mile above sea level and were mosquito friendly.

After faithfully taking my anti-malaria medicine for two years, I ignored it while enjoying the trip home.

Back in Michigan, the problem started with headaches, fever and chills, common enough ailments to initially slough off.

The symptoms persisted, however, and spoiled a welcome-home party arranged by some college friends. I was to be the guest of honor but spent the party time shaking and shivering under a blanket in a bedroom.

"You were too ill … to get out of bed so—as guests arrived— we would parade them into the bedroom for a viewing," one of the hosts, Earl W. Cornett, now a retired Michigan educator, recalled in an email.

The diagnosis, as was the case with the Dallas patient, was not immediate. It took visits to three or four hospitals before the correct call was made, and that was only with the intervention of a doctor who was a family friend. Hospitals can be chaotic places, and malaria was hardly a common diagnosis in Michigan. I don't exactly know what a near-death experience is, but at one point as my temperature spiked, I began to think that living to see another day was unlikely.

One encounter at an emergency room in my hometown of Flint where I was turned away particularly upset my mother. The doctor theorized that I was suffering from effects of drug abuse. My mother had known the doctor for years and never forgave him. While I had my vices, drug abuse was not among them.

The other Flint hospital where the correct diagnosis finally was made was less middle class. It always had reminded me of St. Elsewhere from the old TV series. The place was old and had a reputation as the place where victims of shooting and mayhem seemed to turn up. For me, it turned out to be the place with the best doctors. I will always be grateful to them.

As my recovery proceeded, I became a star patient, with doctors and medical students, some from out of town, stopping by to check my blood.

Where Christians and Muslims Coexist[*]

THE NEWS THAT Ethiopian Christians in 2015 are among the latest murder victims of the terrorist Islamic State, some by beheading and others by shooting, was personal, almost too horrible to bear as I recalled my own experience with Ethiopians of different faiths who coexisted peacefully in the small town where I lived more than 40 years ago.

The Ethiopian murder victims were reported to be impoverished laborers, desperate for work. They had made their way nearly 2,000 miles from their homes in East Africa to Libya, in North Africa along the Mediterranean Sea. They sought work, perhaps in the oil fields, but instead met deaths too brutal and barbaric even to think about. Christians from other countries, including Egypt, were also slain by the terrorists.

The Ethiopians I knew lived in Dabat, a small town in northern Ethiopia where I served as a Peace Corps volunteer from 1968 to 1970.

---

[*] © William Hershey, Akron Beacon Journal, USA Today Network, April 21, 2015.

Although Ethiopian Christianity dates to the fourth century CE, the country during my Peace Corps years and now is a nation where different religions are practiced and tolerated. Currently, about 43.5% of the population identifies with the Christian Ethiopian Orthodox Church while another 33.9% embraces Islam, with other religions making up the balance, according to U.S. government statistics.

My identification with coexistence was firsthand. My housemate was Shumbeza, a teacher who was a Christian. It was common for teachers to provide assistance to needy students in terms of money or food, and Shumbeza aided Kemal, a Muslim. Kemal did not live with us but was frequently at our home. I don't recall a dispute about religion, although my superficial knowledge of Amharic, the official Ethiopian language, could have limited my observations.

The school's faculty was predominantly Christian, but Mohammed, an outgoing, friendly teacher, was embraced by the other teachers as a friend and colleague and participated fully in our frequent social gatherings and fiercely contested games of volleyball.

There were, to be fair, signs of friction beneath the veneer of good will. One of my heroes was Laaka, the assistant school director during one of the years I taught. Although the student body included Christian and Muslim students, we recited a Christian prayer each morning during flag-raising ceremonies.

Laaka, who would have made the ACLU proud, questioned the appropriateness of such a ritual for a student body that was both Muslim and Christian but was overruled.

Students of different faiths got along fine for the most part, anyway.

"There was no distinction between Muslim and Christian," said Abraham, one of my former students who came to the United States after the revolution that deposed Haile Selassie as Ethiopia's emperor in 1974.

Muslims and Christians accommodated each other, Abraham said. At wedding celebrations, for example, there was separate meat for Muslims and Christians.

We all, however, drank from the same supply of tella, the local beer.

In our town, there were Muslims who were native Ethiopians and also Muslims from Arabic countries. The Arabs generally were merchants.

One of my good friends was Tefela. He was from Yemen and owned a small store. He liked to practice his English on me—I was the only American in town.

It was a great honor when Tefela invited me to his home to eat an evening meal, but there was speculation about what would be served as Tefela was Muslim, and I was Christian.

He solved the problem with ease. We had eggs, and they tasted fine.

These buildings in Gondar (*left, above,* and *below*), dating to the 17th century and Emperor Fasilides, are part of the fortress city of Fasil Ghebbi, a UNESCO World Heritage Site. The fortress city includes palaces, churches, monasteries, and other public and private buildings. Fasil Ghebbi served as the center of Ethiopian government from 1636 to 1864.

Celebrating Meskel in Addis Ababa (*above* and *below*). This September holiday for Ethiopian Orthodox Christians commemorates the finding of the True Cross on which Jesus Christ was crucified. According to legend, the cross was found in the fourth century by Helena, mother of Roman Emperor Constantine. She was told in a dream to make a bonfire, and smoke would show her the location of the cross. She lit the bonfire, and smoke rose up and returned to the ground where the cross was buried. Meskel is from the Ge'ez language used in the Ethiopian Orthodox Christian church and translates to "cross."

Clark Hershey and William Hershey leaving Fasil Ghebbi in Gondar in a horse-drawn taxi.

Aderajew Beyene, an eighth-grade student, speaking at United Nations Day at Dabat School. Aderajew came to the United States as a refugee and changed his first name to Abraham, which was easier for Americans to pronounce. He lives with his family in the Atlanta area.

Students celebrating United Nations Day at Dabat School (*above* and *below*).

This funeral (*above* and *below*) for a leading citizen of Dabat drew hundreds of mourners. Musicians played masinkos, traditional stringed instruments.

Loading the bus in Dabat.

Bus driver fixing a flat tire.

Farmer plowing a field near Dabat (*above* and *below*).

Woman along a road near Debarek carrying sticks that provided fuel for cooking fires.

Hershey with students and other teachers playing basketball while crowd looks on.

Butchering a sheep outside Hershey's house.

Boy Scouts and leaders on trip through Simien Mountains (*above* and *below).*

Holiday program in Dabat with local leader speaking and Emperor Haile Selassie's portrait on the wall.

Dabat students on parade.

Dagnew, a teacher at Dabat School, in traditional dress.

Woman in traditional dress.

Woman in traditional dress with her children.

Shepherd boy on road near Debarek with Simien Mountains in background.

Teachers at Debarek School.

Main buildings of Dabat School.

Girma (*left*), Hershey and Bahru on trip to Blue Nile Falls near Bahir Dar. Girma and Bahru were university students assigned to a year of teaching at Dabat School.

Girma (*left*) and Bahru (*squatting*) with guides at Blue Nile Falls near Bahir Dar.

Blue Nile Falls near Bahir Dar.

Doing the laundry in Lake Tana near Bahir Dar.

Tukul, a traditional house made of wood, straw and mud, near
Debarek.

Girl carrying baby on her back on street outside Hershey's house.

Kids playing along the road in Dabat.

Boys playing outside Hershey's house in Dabat.

Kids gathered in front of Hershey's cook house. Meals were cooked in a building separate from the residence.

Hershey (*left*) with dog Barino, Aderajew (hand on Hammer the horse), Shumbeza (*squatting*) and Kemal (*right*) in Dabat. Shumbeza, a teacher, was Hershey's housemate. Aderajew, a student, lived with them. Kemal, also a student, did not live with them, but Shumbeza helped support him.

Clark Hershey (*in hat*), Shumbeza, Alebachew (*squatting*) with dog Barino and Sisay on Dabat School grounds. Sisay and Alebachew were students who lived with Hershey.

Hershey on horse Hammer with Alebachew, a student who lived with Hershey.

Girl students from Debarek School resting.

A volleyball game at Debarek School.

Alebachew (*left*), Hershey and Sisay in front of Hershey's house. Alebachew and Sisay were students who lived with Hershey.

Abebe Kirkos. Abebe, 67, was Hershey's eighth-grade student in Dabat School. He graduated from a two-year course for teachers and taught for seven years in elementary schools. He later earned a bachelor's degree in statistics from Addis Ababa University and also a post graduate diploma in statistics from Makerere University in Kampala, Uganda. He is married and lives in Addis Ababa.

How We Sided with Change in Ethiopia[*]

PRESIDENT DONALD TRUMP's outspoken support for the protesters in Iran brought back memories of half a century ago when hundreds of Peace Corps teachers in Ethiopia, including me, were confronted with a dilemma.

For Trump, the concern is that the president's bellicose tweets could backfire and give Iranian authorities an excuse to blame the protests on the Americans, still regarded as evil even by some critics of the regime.

In Ethiopia, the challenge was whether to stick to our assigned tasks—mostly teaching English, a key to further education and jobs—or to provide our students with a vision of a society that could provide more freedom and opportunities than theirs. As the only foreigner on the faculty, I mostly stuck to teaching but managed to pull off a dirty clothes subterfuge.

* © William Hershey, Akron Beacon Journal, USA Today Network, January 6, 2018.

More about that later.

When we landed in Addis Ababa in 1968, we were transported back in time to a feudal regime ruled by Emperor Haile Selassie.

The emperor's picture was everywhere, in public buildings, bars and restaurants. He was not just Haile Selassie, but His Imperial Majesty Haile Selassie.

The Ethiopian government had a veneer of democracy, including an elected parliament. Haile Selassie, a hero to many around the world for his country's resistance to Italy in World War II, had initiated efforts at modernization, including providing education to a largely illiterate populace.

Still, the emperor and his allies lived lives of unbelievable luxury in a country where many people struggled to survive.

Our guidance from Peace Corps officials was clear. We were guests of the Ethiopian government, feudal or not, and encouraged to keep political opinions to ourselves.

The Cold War was also a factor.

Ethiopia was an American ally in a region where other nations supported communism and the Soviet Union. No reason for a bunch of foreign do-gooders to upset a friend.

There had been protests by Ethiopian university students, but they had been met with strong resistance. In our small, traditional town, located about 500 miles from Addis Ababa, a student who objected to the way things were would have had his or her education ended promptly.

Still, even in this pre-internet era, shortwave radio brought news of the outside world, including stories of political upheavals.

The students and especially the teachers wanted to learn all they could about what was going on outside Ethiopia.

The Ethiopian teachers and I sometimes discussed how things were in Ethiopia and how they would like them to be. They were especially interested in a book, "Ethiopia: A New Political History." It detailed a failed 1960 coup aimed at toppling Haile Selassie and replacing imperial rule with a more representative government.

The book had been banned in Ethiopia, but the teachers knew about it and were eager to get their hands on a copy.

That's where the dirty clothes subterfuge came in. During a vacation to the East African nations of Kenya, Uganda, and Tanzania, I bought several copies of the books for the teachers.

The Ethiopian authorities were on the outlook for such seditious material. To evade customs inspectors, I hid the books among my dirty clothes when I returned to Ethiopia, and they went undetected.

The teachers got their books, and I hope that I signaled that I sympathized with their desire for change.

President Trump could try a more indirect or even behind-the-scenes approach than nasty tweets to show support for the Iranian protesters.

That, of course, is not the preferred approach for somebody who likes to say, "You're fired."

If he tries, the ayatollahs won't pay much attention.

An Emperor, a Governor, and a President[*]

HIS IMPERIAL MAJESTY Haile Selassie I, the former Ethiopian emperor, and James A. Rhodes, the former Ohio governor, didn't have much in common.

Taken together, however, they've helped me focus on President Donald Trump's mean-spirited and violence-inspiring attacks on journalists.

I caught glimpses of the emperor several times at parades and ceremonies during the two years I served as a Peace Corps teacher in Ethiopia from 1968–1970.

It wasn't easy.

At 5'2", he could be hard to spot.

Trump may aspire to be the first American autocrat, but the emperor was the real thing. His picture was everywhere, in schools, hotels, restaurants and private homes.

* © William Hershey, Akron Beacon Journal, USA Today Network, August 9, 2018.

Notice that I didn't refer to him as "Haile Selassie." It had to be "His Imperial Majesty Haile Selassie I."

Even more properly, it was His Imperial Majesty Haile Selassie I, Conquering Lion of the Tribe of Judah, King of Kings and Elect of God.

He received the kind of press coverage that Trump believes he deserves. The pages of the Ethiopian Herald were filled with flattering pictures of the diminutive emperor, decked out in military regalia, along with stories praising all that he was doing for his country.

In his book, "The Emperor: Downfall of an Autocrat," author Ryszard Kapuściński describes the deference shown to the emperor, deference that Trump so longs for.

Kapuściński interviewed a servant who helped with the emperor's dog, Lulu: "He (Lulu) was allowed to sleep in the Emperor's great bed. During various ceremonies, he would run away from the Emperor's lap and pee on dignitaries' shoes. The august gentlemen were not allowed to flinch or make the slightest gesture when they felt their feet getting wet. I had to walk among the dignitaries and wipe the urine from their shoes with a satin cloth. This was my job for 10 years."

Unlike the emperor, Rhodes was not born to royalty but to humble beginnings in Coalton in Jackson County in southern Ohio coal country.

He shared one thing with Trump—adoring Fox News-like coverage.

In their book, "James A. Rhodes: Ohio Colossus," authors Tom Diemer, Lee Leonard and Richard G. Zimmerman describe the coverage Rhodes received from the Columbus Dispatch for much of his political career: "From the time Rhodes was mayor (of Columbus), the Wolfe-owned Columbus Evening Dispatch was his unabashed supporter, both on the editorial page and in its news columns."

The cheerleading coverage from the Dispatch eased off toward the end of Rhodes's career, but he already had figured out how to deal with reporters from other news outlets.

Rhodes, the only Ohioan elected to four four-year terms as governor, was the Muhammad Ali of the press conference—bobbing, weaving and occasionally hiding in the weeds.

His skill at manipulating exposes Trump's weakness, not strength, in dealing with reporters. Rhodes knew that he had more information than the reporters. He toyed with us, doling out newsy tidbits when he felt like it but saw no reason to demonize. He preferred to throw out popcorn balls and serve hamburgers from Wendy's, in which he had invested and profited.

Bill Cohen, the longtime Statehouse reporter for public radio, pursued Rhodes as doggedly as CNN's Jim Acosta goes after Trump, although without the same self-righteous zeal.

Rhodes, governor from 1963–1970 and 1975–1982, called Cohen "Cronkite" and kept talking in disjointed sentences.

A Rhodes's specialty was dodging questions about an upcoming gubernatorial appointment. The exchanges went something like this:

"Governor, are you considering Fred Jones?"

"Maybe."

"How about Jane Brown?"

"She has some good points."

"Ed Johnson?"

"Could be."

We usually didn't know who Rhodes was considering until he made the appointment.

He even knew how to handle the national press, something Trump hasn't mastered. These reporters are smart and hard-working but often patronizing, pompous and parochial. Unlike Trump, Rhodes didn't mock or threaten them.

He just outsmarted them.

When they visited Ohio with Republican presidents or presidential candidates, they guffawed as Rhodes talked about *feeshing* and pounded the podium with his wallet to emphasize pocketbook issues.

As I recall, he helped them with the pronunciation of George H. W. Bush.

"That's *Boosh*," Rhodes explained. "B-o-o-s-h."

Rhodes's ability to manipulate press coverage wasn't a civic virtue.

Still, Trump could learn from Rhodes, who died at 91 in 2001.

The president is too smart to learn anything from anybody, but reporters should be wary if Trump hears about the Ethiopian emperor and starts bringing a dog to his press conferences.

Where Are the Welcome and the Hope?[*]

THE ONGOING LEGAL battle over President Donald Trump's executive order temporarily shutting America's door to refugees and citizens of seven Muslim-majority countries takes me back nearly 50 years to my arrival for Peace Corps training in 1968 in the small Ethiopian city of Nazret.

One of Nazret's popular bars was named after President John Kennedy.

The decision to name that bar after an American president, better than any civics lesson, reflected the reputation the United States had in Ethiopia and around much of the world as a welcoming beacon of hope.

What a contrast it was to Trump's desire to roll up the nation's welcome mat and shut out the world.

My arrival in Nazret came five years after President Kennedy's assassination and seven years after his inaugural

---

* © William Hershey, Akron Beacon Journal, USA Today Network, February 16, 2017.

address sent a message that still reverberated in Ethiopia and around the world:

"We shall pay any price, bear any burden, meet any hardship, support any friend, oppose any foe to assure the survival and success of liberty."

By 1968 some of the glow had dimmed from President Kennedy's inspiring words with the assassinations of Dr. Martin Luther King Jr., the nation's leading civil rights leader, and the president's own brother Robert.

The Vietnam War, the Watergate scandal and the humiliation of the Iranian hostage crisis plunged the nation into more than a decade of self-doubt.

There had been tough times before—a Civil War, the Great Depression and World War II fought on two continents. The nation has been resilient.

President Kennedy was a Democrat, but in those days the nation's optimistic resolve was bipartisan. Another president, Republican Ronald Reagan, came along to take the torch from Kennedy. Reagan was elected in 1980 and overwhelmingly reelected in 1984.

Republicans who embrace Trump's insular worldview and his bellicose insults and threats to Mexicans and others should listen to how Reagan described our nation in his farewell address in 1989:

"After 200 years, two centuries, she still stands strong and true to the granite ridge, and her glow has held no matter what storm. And she's still a beacon, still a magnet for all who must have freedom, for all the pilgrims from all the lost places who are hurtling through the darkness, toward home."

This embrace of America's special and sometimes dangerous role in the world continued with the presidency of George H. W. Bush, who finished off Reagan's determination to end the Cold War with the downfall of global communism.

Next, Democratic President Bill Clinton, after a hesitant start, continued America's willingness to take a leading role in defusing global trouble spots by helping stop the ethnic cleansing that had turned the Balkans into a killing ground.

It was another Republican president, however, who showed that even in our darkest hour the United States does not turn its back on people whose religion made them easy targets of suspicion.

Just days after September 11, 2001, when Al-Qaeda terrorists in four hijacked planes killed nearly 3,000 Americans, President George W. Bush visited a mosque to speak out against mistreatment of Arabs and Muslims and the need to understand, not condemn, Islam.

"The face of terror is not the true faith of Islam. That's not what Islam is about," Bush said. "Islam is peace. These terrorists don't represent peace. They represent evil and war."

We are living again in troubling times, and there is no certainty how the history of this era will be written.

One thing, however, seems almost certain: no bar in Nazret, Ethiopia, is likely to be named after President Trump.

Plumber, Taxi Driver Tell America's Story[*]

JOE THE PLUMBER, meet Abraham the taxi driver. Joe's familiar to most Americans by now. He became a fixture of the 2008 presidential campaign and campaigned for Republican John McCain.

Joe—actually Samuel Joseph Wurzelbacher—met up with Democrat Barack Obama in suburban Toledo last month and bashed Obama's tax plan. Wurzelbacher believes it would hurt his chances to buy the plumbing business he works for.

Joe's aspirations to become a small business owner represent an important part of America's story.

Businesspeople who started out with less than Joe have created millions of jobs, made themselves rich and helped make the United States the economic envy of the world, even in these tough economic times.

* "Plumber, Taxi Driver Tell American's Story," William Hershey, Dayton Daily News, Cox First Media, November 2, 2008.

Democrats don't agree with Joe's analysis of Obama's and McCain's tax plans, but if they're smart, they won't beat up on his dream.

Abraham also represents a part of the American story, a part that probably doesn't get talked about enough in the onslaught of attack ads and celebrity Get Out the Vote rock-fests that dominate the campaign for president.

It's a part that immigrants like Abraham, who came here from Ethiopia in January 1982, with literally nothing but the clothes on his back, can see clearer than the rest of us—the power to change things by voting.

I know Abraham—Abraham Beyene—better than Joe. He was my student 40 years ago in an Ethiopian school when I was a Peace Corps teacher.

My wife and I helped bring him to Ohio from Sudan with the help of two churches. He had fled there on foot after fighting in Ethiopia's bloody civil struggles that erupted after Emperor Haile Selassie was deposed in 1974.

After graduating from Ohio State in 1987, Abraham moved to the Atlanta area. Like Joe, he looked for better economic opportunities. He landed a job with a land development company but when hard times hit, and he was laid off, he started driving a taxi.

These days, he's still driving and also helping his wife Tirue raise their son Bruck, 15, and daughter Seday, 12. The family's day starts at 3:30 a.m. when Tirue gets up for her job at a grocery-store bakery. Abraham drives the kids to school and then heads to the airport to pick up some fares.

He's taken a separate job this year—registering voters. He registered some at an Ethiopian festival and then took more forms to the airport where he signed up about 29 taxi drivers. Like him, most were immigrants—Ethiopians, Somalis, Pakistanis, Indians and Iranians.

"If any American doesn't see any country outside of his own nation, then he wouldn't take the voting rights seriously," Abraham said. "To people like me who have been deprived of those rights or people like South Africans who sacrificed their lives to get voting power, it means a lot."

He tells his son Bruck that voting matters.

"All your life is affected by elected officials, your gas bill, your mortgage, your water bill, your electric bill, the schools, the day-care centers, the health system," Abraham said.

He supports Obama for president but backed Hillary Clinton in the Democratic primary, partly because of her husband Bill.

"I bought my house during this period of his presidency. I had good money. The economy was good. The country was at peace. The guy was for the middle class and the lower class," he said.

Also, he didn't think American voters were ready to pick a Black man like Obama to run for president.

"The outcome changed my mind," he said. "He (Obama) defeated all the odds." Obama's a long shot in Georgia, but Abraham is not deterred. "There's no perfection in the world," he said. "Things are relative."

The Letter of Hope*

MOST LETTERS TO the Akron Regional Development Board (ARDB) seek information about starting a business in the Akron area.

This one, dated February 8, 1981, was different.

"Dear Sir," it began. "I'm sure you have concluded that I'm dead." It was addressed to me, care of the ARDB, from Aderajew Beyene, one of my students when I was a Peace Corps volunteer in Ethiopia.

Ad (pronounced Odd) was a refugee in the Sudan, Ethiopia's neighbor to the west, where he had fled on foot from the Marxist military government that had toppled Ethiopian Emperor Haile Selassie I in 1974.

The trip had taken two months and zigzagged over hundreds of miles across often rugged Ethiopian terrain. To avoid detection, Ad and about 100 other refugees traveled at night.

---

* © William Hershey, Akron Beacon Journal, Beacon Magazine, USA Today Network, June 7, 1987.

When Kim Garner, then an ARDB research assistant, opened the letter, it was a crucial step in a remarkable journey that led to Ohio Stadium in Columbus, where Ad graduated on June 12, 1987, at Ohio State's 300th commencement with a bachelor's degree in economic geography and urban studies.

The trip had started years before for Ad. As a boy of about 10, wanting more out of life than herding sheep and goats, he fled his father and started going to school.

At first, there was help from relatives, Ethiopian teachers, and fellow students. Later, when his trip seemed at a dead end, assistance came from Akron's First Presbyterian Church on E. Market Street, a Presbyterian Church refugee specialist in New York, a U.S. embassy official in the Sudan, an unnamed American doctor who treated Ad for malaria while he was a refugee, and retired Nationwide Insurance executive Dean Jeffers in Columbus, among many others.

"So would you please share my problem in finding his address," Ad wrote.

"I wasn't thinking about going to college," Ad recalled recently. "The primary task was to save the life."

The envelope from the Sudan actually contained two letters. One was to me and my family. The other, a cover letter, desperately requested that the second letter be sent to me.

"So would you please share my problem in finding his address (*sic*)?" Ad wrote. After arriving in the Sudan, Ad had tried to find me and my family through the Peace Corps and the United Nations, but he had no luck. An American doctor treating him for malaria at a refugee center suggested that he try again by writing to me in care of the chamber of commerce in Akron.

Ad will never knock the often-maligned U.S. Postal Service. There has been no chamber of commerce in Akron for years, but someone in the post office knew that the ARDB had taken over the chamber's job and sent Ad's letter there.

That's where Garner came in. She treated Ad's letter like any other. Instead of providing information on business locations, however, she called the Beacon Journal and found out that I was assigned to the Columbus bureau.

"We recently received this letter from a gentleman who claims he met you overseas and lost contact several years ago due to political problems in his country...I hope this comes as a pleasant surprise," she wrote in a letter that arrived just a few days later at the Beacon Journal's Columbus bureau.

My wife Marica and I had, in fact, feared Ad was dead. We last saw him in 1973 when we returned to Ethiopia to train new Peace Corps volunteers. Marcia also had been a Peace Corps teacher in Ethiopia in 1968–1970 in a town close to mine in central Ethiopia. We met there and married soon after returning to the United States.

On our return in 1973, we took along our daughter Laura, just two. Ad was one of the reasons we decided we could make the trip with a young child. As an eighth grader, he had lived with me and my Ethiopian roommate Shumbeza, also a teacher. Ad was not only the school's best student, but a hard and responsible worker around the house.

His job in 1973 was taking care of Laura. Among other things, that meant handwashing her diapers nearly every day. Laura, now 16, and Ad laugh about that now.

We left Ad at the end of the summer in 1973 and returned to Ohio, keeping in touch by letter as he graduated from a teacher-training high school (a college education wasn't required to teach in Ethiopia) and began a career.

The revolution of 1974, however, made corresponding dangerous. The new military government refined itself by bloody purges. Anti-Americanism was its trademark. Soviet advisers and Cuban troops flooded Ethiopia.

By 1977, our family, which by then included Patrick, our son, lost touch with Ad. He explained this in his cover letter to the ARDB:

"I was forced to stop writing them for the fascist junta was anti-American and was torturing those who were exchanging letters with Americans."

Ad's letter to us unleashed a flood of emotions. First was thanksgiving that he was alive. But there was sadness, too. Many young Ethiopians literally had begged to come with us to the United States. Ad was never like that. He seemed determined to make a career for himself and help his proud, but in many ways backward, country struggle into the 20th century. It seemed to us that the role of the Peace Corps was to help young persons such as Ad develop their own countries, not to skim the cream of a country's elite by resettling them in the United States.

Ad had been mostly on his own since he started school in the mid-1960s. He was about ten then, but meticulous birth records weren't kept in the countryside where Ad was born, so his exact age is uncertain.

He got the idea of going to school from his cousins who walked about four miles each way to Dabat.

Ad's father had no use for school, particularly for his eldest son who eventually was supposed to take over farming.

A fierce traditionalist, Ad's father even objected that his son was a natural left-hander. Most Ethiopian dishes are eaten by hand. Tradition has it that the food is blessed only when eaten with the right hand.

When Ad started eating with his left hand, his father cut slits in the fingers of Ad's left hand, which made eating that way painful, if not impossible. (This hurt a little, but not as much, Ad said, as having his tonsils removed by the local medicine man while Ad was still conscious.)

Later, his father would walk to Dabat and urge teachers not to permit Ad to write left-handed.

When Ad started school, he was placed in second grade. After the first year his father kicked him out of the house, and he was on his own. He lived with an uncle for a while, then a grandmother, and in the seventh grade with students from the countryside who rented a room in Dabat and let Ad join them without paying.

Sometimes he stretched propriety a bit.

In the seventh grade, for example, Ad needed money at exam time. The daughter of a local saloon owner had money, but bad study habits. Ad wrote his own history final left-handed then shifted the pencil to his right hand to do her test. He earned $2, more than enough for a day's worth of meals, but was caught by the teacher, who let him off with a warning.

As a refugee in the Sudan, Ad needed more than his wits to escape.

We wanted to help and first turned to friends who were Presbyterian ministers, Harry Van Fleet of the First Presbyterian Church in Akron, where we still were members, and Kent Organ, a church administrator in Cleveland who had been our pastor when we lived in Dayton. We also wrote to Senator John Glenn, whose staff later helped guide us through the resettlement maze.

Van Fleet and Organ referred us to the Presbyterian Church's New York office for world relief, emergency, and resettlement services. By mid-March we were in touch with Anne Walline, a specialist in resettlement services.

Our willingness to sponsor Ad's resettlement in the United States didn't mean he could immediately get on a plane and head for Columbus. First, Ad had to be "located" by the United Nations High Commissioner for Refugees' office in the Sudan to determine his interest in getting to the United States. Then he had to be interviewed by American embassy and immigration officials to determine if he deserved to resettle here.

With thousands of Ethiopian refugees in Khartoum, the Sudan capital, none of this was easy.

A big break came after we wrote to the U.S. ambassador in the Sudan on March 20, 1981. We soon received a reply from Robert Boehme, the vice consul who arranged to interview Ad.

All the time, we kept in touch with Ad. We told him that it was important to convince American officials that he feared for his life if he returned to Ethiopia and that he steadfastly opposed the Marxist, military government in Ethiopia.

He took little convincing. Like many young Ethiopians, Ad at first supported the revolution. Despite Haile Selassie's international reputation as a kind of benign despot, his government had been corrupt, repressive, and insensitive to the needs of the majority of the people. He lived off the fat of generous American aid and reportedly stored up riches for himself and his family in foreign banks.

When famine struck part of Ethiopia in the early 1970s, his unwillingness—or inability—to respond, coupled with growing dissatisfaction with his one-man rule, brought him down. The United States, preoccupied with Vietnam, chose not to help him.

Gradually, however, the new ruling junta pursued a reign of terror. Ad and many other young, educated Ethiopians became disillusioned. They had traded one dictatorship for a crueler one.

Haile Selassie's troops, Ad recalled, had killed student protesters at the university in Addis Ababa, but the new government "not only killed students, it killed children, regardless of sex or age."

By 1978, Ad found himself under house arrest in a small town in central Ethiopia. The local Communist Party officials had objected to the way he taught Marxist-Leninist theory.

In 1979, he escaped and joined one of the guerrilla movements scattered all over the country. By June 15, 1980, a date he remembers well, he decided to leave Ethiopia and began his hike out of the country.

It was just short of a year later that Boehme, the vice consul at the American embassy, wrote us about his interview with Ad. Boehme said Ad's case for resettlement—based on fear for his life if he returned to Ethiopia—was a "persuasive one" and that a "favorable opinion" from immigration officials was likely.

Despite Boehme's optimism, the next few months were frustrating. There were delays in getting Ad officially identified as a refugee by United Nations officials and then getting his case passed on to American and church officials for resettlement.

Through Walline in New York, we had signed on to be Ad's sponsors, which meant we would help him resettle once he arrived in the United States. The United States Refugee Program would lend him the money for the flight here. (Ad has since paid back the $540 lent him for the trip.)

As the summer turned into early fall, however, Walline cautioned that it might be a good idea for us to have a church as an "institutional sponsor" to show there would be financial backup for Ad in case of an emergency. We tried a church in Columbus that we were attending, but the leaders weren't interested.

On October 2, we decided to try First Presbyterian Church in Akron. Art Sutton, then chairman of the Mission Administration Committee, stated our case and the church became Ad's "institutional sponsor."

That sponsorship seemed somehow to be the catalyst that moved Ad's case along. On October 13, we received a letter from Walline with this good news:

"Here at long last is the copy of the bio we have received for your friend . . . proof that he has become a case and will proceed as one from now on."

The bio was the news Walline had been waiting for. It set in motion the final steps that put Ad on an airplane that took him to New York on January 28 and then to Columbus the next day, where we met him. He was unprepared for the Ohio winter, wearing cloth shoes and only a sweater for a wrap.

"I felt secure," Ad recalled of his arrival in the United States. "It was just like a rebirth." After a few days at our house, Ad moved in with some Ethiopians we had befriended and started looking for a job. That was a problem. He understood spoken English but was a little rusty when it came to making himself understood.

By May, he still had no job.

"It was frustrating," he recalled. "I don't want to be a burden. I want to make my own life." That's where Dean Jeffers, the retired general chairman and chief executive officer of Nationwide Insurance came in. I had met Jeffers while preparing a Beacon Magazine article on his friend, John Galbreath, the Columbus builder, and sportsman. Jeffers was not only well connected in Columbus but seemed like the type of person willing to help somebody such as Ad with no expectation of being paid back.

So, I called him and briefly explained the problem. He gave me the name of an official at Wendy's, the Columbus-based fast-food chain. Within days, Ad went for an interview and on May 19 started work.

While working at Wendy's, Ad went back to school to get a high school diploma. He received it in the fall of 1982 and in the spring of 1983 began his studies at Ohio State.

Since then, he's switched jobs and now works at Grant Hospital in the food-service department. Last June he bought a used car, an achievement that still amazes him.

"I came without nothing," he said. "I had only a pair of pants. I started from scratch." Ad still gets lonely for his family, particularly his mother, who neither reads nor writes but loves her son.

"She understands where I am," he said. "She wants to see me before she dies." The chain of circumstances that allowed him to get out of the Sudan and come to the United States sometimes seems incredible to him.

"I didn't think I would (make) contact with you," he said of his letter that reached the ARDB. "I was curious how the government would care for a single letter and find out (where it should go.)"

These are said to be uncertain times in the United States, but Ad doesn't brood about the future. "It's optimistic. It's bright. I did just what I wanted to do. I take my problems one at a time. Now, I just want to graduate.

"I know my education will give me something beneficial."

Postscript
Aderajew moved to the Atlanta area after graduation. He changed his first name to Abraham because it is easier for Americans to pronounce. He took a job in land development but was laid off. He became a cab driver and retired after 17 years. He and his wife Tirue have two children, Bruck, 28, an electrical engineer, and Seday, 25, a graphic designer.

A Refugee Story about America[*]

PRESIDENT DONALD TRUMP'S efforts to shut America's doors to the world's persecuted, homeless, and forgotten don't represent the kind of country I want to live in.

A recent meeting in Columbus with Abraham Beyene reminded me that not all Americans share the president's fondness for mocking and demonizing those seeking a better life here.

I had taught Abraham English and math as a Peace Corps volunteer in a small Ethiopian town 50 years ago.

Thanks to a collection of open-hearted Americans, my wife Marcia and I were able to bring Abraham to the United States after he fled Ethiopia to escape the brutal Marxist military regime that took over the country after Emperor Haile Selassie was deposed in 1974.

Abraham, who lives in the Atlanta area, was visiting Columbus for a wedding when our discussion turned to his path to American citizenship.

---

* © William Hershey, Akron Beacon Journal, USA Today Network, August 1, 2019.

We talked just as Trump was denouncing four Democratic congresswomen, all women of color, and suggesting they "go back" to "the totally broken and crime-infested places from which they came."

Three of the women—Rashida Tlaib of Michigan, Alexandra Ocasio-Cortez of New York, and Ayanna Pressley of Massachusetts—were born in the United States.

The fourth—Ilhan Omar of Minnesota—is a naturalized citizen who fled Somalia and came to the United States after a stop in Kenya.

While Trump's attacks grabbed the headlines, his real anti-refugee work goes on with less fanfare.

According to the United Nations High Commissioner for Refugees, the world is experiencing the highest level ever of displaced persons. Of nearly 25.9 million refugees, more than half are younger than 18.

Trump, however, has declared the United States "full" and set the number of refugees permitted this fiscal year at 30,000, a historic low. The Obama administration had set the number for 2017 at 100,000. Trump reduced it to 50,000. The cap for 2018 was 45,000.

This does not reflect the magical cooperation that resulted in Abraham reaching America.

He had become strongly opposed to Ethiopia's Marxist military government and in 1979 joined a guerrilla movement fighting it.

By 1980, however, he decided to flee Ethiopia. He joined a group that walked hundreds of miles through rugged terrain to neighboring Sudan and ended up in Khartoum, the capital.

His first break came when he went to a clinic for treatment of malaria. He asked an American doctor how to get in touch with Marcia and me. The doctor suggested he write us care of the chamber of commerce in Akron.

He did. His letter ended up at the Akron Regional Development Board where a research assistant found out that I worked in the Beacon Journal's Columbus bureau and forwarded the letter there.

"Dear sir," it began. "I'm sure you have concluded that I'm dead." The letter ignited a flurry of phone calls and letters to Senator John Glenn, two friends who were Presbyterian ministers and others. Glenn's staff and church officials helped guide us through the resettlement maze.

Glenn, who died at 95 in 2016, apparently added a personal touch, which Abraham recalled during his recent visit.

Marcia and I wanted to sponsor Abraham for resettlement in the United States but there were many hoops to go through. Among them, he had to have an interview at the American embassy.

Embassy officials learned of Abraham from the people and groups helping us but an embassy official told me in a letter than they had not been able to locate him.

Abraham told me that he went to the embassy in person to seek an interview but was turned away. He tried a second time, however, and got unexpected help.

Our Peace Corps service had ended in 1970, but Marcia and I returned to Ethiopia in 1973 to train new volunteers. Abraham lived with us during training and helped care for our young daughter Laura. He got to know the trainees.

Back in Khartoum, as he waited outside the American embassy Abraham heard the voices of two of the volunteers we had trained in 1973. They were in the Sudan for academic research. They recognized Abraham, and he told them that he needed to see the ambassador.

They arranged for a visit. Abraham handed the ambassador a note from me introducing him.

The ambassador then produced a letter from Senator Glenn that apparently explained Abraham's situation.

"He (the ambassador) rose up from his chair, firmly shook my hand and told me he was looking for me all over the city," Abraham told me in an email.

That meeting helped set in motion the process by which Abraham was designated as a refugee. First Presbyterian Church in Akron joined us in sponsoring him, and he arrived in Columbus on January 29, 1982, and eventually became a naturalized citizen.

He moved to Atlanta and married an Ethiopian woman who joined him there. Abraham's now a retired cab driver while his wife works as a cook in a senior citizens' development. They have two adult children.

He does not care much for Trump, but has fond memories of President John F. Kennedy, who he heard about as a boy over shortwave radio, and of Senator Glenn. His email summed up his feelings for the country that took him in:

"God bless America."

Ethiopia: Profile of a Nation

ETHIOPIAN EMPEROR HAILE Selassie ordered his far-flung subjects to join forces in October of 1935 to repel invaders from Italy:

> Soldiers, group yourselves under your chiefs, obey them with one heart, repulse the invader!
> Those who because of infirmities or feebleness cannot participate actively in this sacred struggle can assist by their prayers.
> The opinion of the whole world is revolted by this unprovoked aggression against Ethiopia.
> God will be with us! Long live the Emperor of Ethiopia!

The emperor's order captured the fierce independence and defiant courage that have been Ethiopian trademarks throughout its long and storied history

The Italian invasion succeeded, but only briefly. Haile Selassie was forced into exile in England in 1936 but, with the help of the British, returned in 1941 as a conquering hero.

Ethiopia, located on the Horn of Africa, succeeded in resisting European colonization, except for that brief Italian occupation. It is the oldest independent nation in Africa and one of the oldest nations in the world. Other African nations looked to Ethiopia for leadership as they struggled to break free from European colonization.

The Organization of African Unity—now the African Union—was established in 1963 in Addis Ababa, where the headquarters remains.

The three colors of the Ethiopian flag—green, red and yellow—were used so often by other African nations upon their independence that they became known as the Pan-African colors.

Rich History

Ethiopia is rich not just in human history, but in prehuman history as well. Hadar in northeastern Ethiopia was the site of a major find in 1974 by American anthropologist Donald Johnson. "Lucy," as the partial skeleton became known, dated back to 3.2 million years ago and was part of *Australopithecus afarensis,* a key link in human evolution.

Humans came along later. Habitation dates to the 10th Century BCE, making it part of one of the world's most continuously populated regions.

By the second century CE, the Kingdom of Axum in northern Ethiopia had become a regional trading power on the Red Sea. There were cultural exchanges and commerce with the Arabian Peninsula that produced the legend of the union of the Queen of Sheba from southwestern Arabia or Ethiopia—her location is disputed—with the Israelite King Solomon. Their union produced Menelik I, who became king of Axum and the founder of what became Ethiopia's royal dynasty. Haile Selassie was the last monarch in the Solomonic line.

Christianity came early to Ethiopia and by the fourth century CE had become the state religion. Ethiopia's most stunning tribute to Christianity may be the 11 churches carved in the ground out of rock in Lalibela in north central Ethiopia. The churches date to around 1200 CE and are a UNESCO World Heritage Site.

Islam also has had a strong presence in Ethiopia, starting around the seventh century CE, and there was rivalry and conflict between Christian and Muslim leaders in the ensuing centuries.

While the embrace of Christianity and Islam gave Ethiopia something in common with other parts of the world, Ethiopian culture and traditions developed in unique ways. Time is even measured differently than in most of the rest of the world.

The Ethiopian calendar has 13 months, not 12. Ethiopia calculates the birth of Jesus Christ differently than other nations, making its calendar seven to eight years behind the Gregorian calendar used by most other countries.

Early in its history, Ethiopia began developing an agriculturally based economy, with coffee one of the cornerstones. Ethiopia is widely considered to be the birthplace of coffee, although other countries also make that claim.

An Ethiopian legend traces the development of coffee to a goat herder named Kaldi in the 9th century CE. He was herding his flock when he noticed that the goats were bleating and dancing around after eating bright red berries. Kaldi tried the berries for himself and, like the goats, felt a jolt of energy. He took the coffee beans to a nearby monastery where the monks at first rejected them as "the Devil's work" and hurled them into the fire. They gave coffee a second chance, however, when the aroma of the beans roasting caught their attention. They removed the beans from the fire, crushed them and covered them with hot water to preserve them. The monks tried out this coffee and found that it kept them awake through prayer and devotions. They pledged to drink this new beverage daily to help their devotions.

Today coffee remains Ethiopia's chief export, with an estimated 15 million Ethiopians relying on coffee for a living. Coffee is part of an agriculture-based economy. Agriculture accounts for 90% of exports and 40% of GDP. More than 70% of the labor force works in agriculture.

Emergence of Modern Ethiopia

Centuries of political and religious rivalries culminated in a violent era that became known as the "Era of the Princes" from 1706 to 1855 as regional rulers battled each other for power. It was under Emperor Tewodros that the outlines of modern Ethiopia began to emerge in 1855. He held the country together mainly by coercion after his efforts at social reform met resistance from the clergy and regional aristocrats. When Queen Victoria of England ignored his offer of an alliance to destroy Islam, Tewodros imprisoned the British envoy and other Europeans.

The English struck back with an Anglo-Indian military expedition in 1868. Sir Robert Napier, the British commander, used money and weapons to gain the support of Kassa, a dejazmatch (earl) in the northern region of Tigray to help his troops move inland. Napier's troops defeated a small Ethiopian force at Amba Maryam in central Ethiopia. Tewodros committed suicide two days after the battle to avoid capture.

After a period of internal conflict, Kassa gained control of the country and took the crown as Yohannes IV in 1872. He became the first Ethiopian ruler in 300 years to have authority over a swath of the country from Tigray in the north to the Gurage region south of what is now Addis Ababa. Emperor Yohannes IV spent much of his time resisting military attacks from Italy, Egypt and Sudan and was killed in battle in 1889.

Yohannes was succeeded by Emperor Menelik II. The new emperor's wife, Taitu, persuaded her husband to make Addis Ababa, located on a verdant, well-watered plateau in the center of the country, the capital. It was the empress who gave the city its name, which means "New Flower."

On the battlefront, Menelik signed a treaty giving Italy control over Eritrea but resisted Italian efforts to control all of Ethiopia. The Italians underestimated the Ethiopian forces. In 1896 the Ethiopians vanquished the Italians at the Battle of Adua. The victory represented the first crushing defeat of a European power by African forces during the colonial era. It is still celebrated every year in Ethiopia.

Menelik expanded Ethiopia to its present size and was succeeded upon his death in 1913 by his grandson Iyasu. Iyasu upset Christians by integrating Muslims into his administration and was deposed in 1916. This paved the way for the ascension of Emperor Haile Selassie I, although that did not happen immediately.

Iyasu at first was replaced by Menelik's daughter, Zewditu. It was not considered proper for a woman to reign in her own right so Ras Tafari, a cousin of Menelik, became Zewditu's regent and heir apparent.

The Conquering Lion of Judah

When Zewditu died in 1930, Ras Tafari declared himself emperor and, as was common for reigning emperors, chose a new name, Haile Selassie I, which means "Power of the Trinity." He was crowned as His Imperial Majesty Haile Selassie I, the Conquering Lion of the Tribe of Judah, King of Kings and Elect of God. Haile Selassie was a small man, just 5 feet 2 inches tall, but as Ethiopia's dominant leader of the 20th century, was recognized globally for his leadership and efforts at African unity.

He began work on roads, schools, hospitals, communications and other public services as Ethiopia began a slow process of modernization and exposure to the global economy.

His efforts collided with the ambitions of Italy's ruler Benito Mussolini to increase Italian influence in the Horn of Africa. As Italian forces attacked Ethiopia and terrorized the civilian population with blasts of mustard gas fired from aircraft in 1935, Haile Selassie commanded his own people to resist the invaders:

Everyone will now be mobilized and all boys old enough to carry a spear will be sent to Addis Ababa. Married men will take their wives to carry food and cook. Those without wives will take any woman without a husband. Women with small babies need not go. The blind, those who cannot walk, or for any reason cannot carry a spear, are exempted. Anyone found at home after the receipt of this order will be hanged.

He also went to Geneva in June of 1936 to plead for help from the League of Nations: "It is to defend a people struggling for its age-old independence that the head of the Ethiopian Empire has come to Geneva to fulfill this supreme duty, after having himself fought at the head of his armies."

He ended with:

"Representatives of the world I have come to Geneva to discharge in your midst the most painful of duties of a head of state. What reply shall I have to take back to my people?"

The league ignored his plea, and the emperor was forced into exile in England in 1936. In 1940 the United Kingdom recognized Haile Selassie as a full ally, and he soon came to Khartoum in Sudan to train a British-led Ethiopian army. On May 5, 1941, Haile Selassie returned to Ethiopia in triumph. In 1952 Eritrea was made part of Ethiopia, giving the empire a coastline on the Red Sea.

Ethiopia under Haile Selassie developed a close relationship with the United States. It became a key American ally in Africa in the Cold War rivalry that developed between the United States and the Soviet Union. Ethiopia was one of the first countries to receive Peace Corps volunteers, with the first 427 arriving in 1962.

Domestically, the emperor continued cautious reforms, including the development of a national system of education and granting limited powers to parliament. The reforms in some ways helped lead to his downfall. When members of the military went abroad for training, they were exposed to representative governments. At the same time students at Haile Selassie I University in Addis Ababa began to explore new ideas, both of western democracy and communism in the Soviet Union and China.

Government administrators charged with carrying out the emperor's modest changes began to envision a society that operated for more than the benefit of the emperor's family and allies.

Haile Selassie's troubles accelerated in 1973 with a drought in two northern provinces that ultimately claimed 100,000 lives and was made worse by government efforts to cover it up. The next year mutinies broke out in the military over low pay. A secessionist guerrilla war in Eritrea caused more problems for Haile Selassie.

Finally, the emperor was deposed by a military coup in September of 1974 and seven months later died at 83 in a small apartment in his former palace. His death at first was attributed to natural causes but evidence later suggested that he had been strangled at the order of the military government.

Continued Instability

Ethiopia had been seen as a symbol of political stability in Africa, but that changed after Haile Selassie was deposed. Violent turmoil followed. First came the Derg, a brutal Marxist military dictatorship. Ethiopia–U.S. relations cooled as the Derg allied itself with the Soviet Union. The Derg ruled until 1991 when it was overthrown by a coalition of rebel forces.

The new government was dominated by the Tigray ethnic group, representing about 6% of the population, and its party, the Tigray People's Liberation Front (TPLF).

Some reforms and economic progress ensued. A constitution was adopted in 1994 that established regionalism and ethnic autonomy as key principles. The nation's first multi-party elections were held in 1995 and Meles Zenawi from the TPLF was elected prime minister.

State-led development under Meles focused on eliminating poverty, improving agriculture, building roads and expanding education and health services throughout the country.

However, there were ethnic disputes and other problems. Eritrea, which had been an Italian colony until becoming part of Ethiopia after World War II, established its independence in 1993 after a referendum. Border disputes between the Ethiopia and Eritrea increased tensions.

Meles died in 2012 and was replaced as prime minister by Hailemariam Desalegn, marking the first peaceful transition of power in decades. By 2015, however, violent anti-government protests began, and in 2018 Hailemariam resigned. He was replaced by Abiy Ahmed Ali, Ethiopia's first prime minister from the nation's largest ethnic group, the Oromo.

There was initial optimism as the new prime minister initiated political reforms and released political prisoners. Following the settlement of the border dispute with Eritrea, Abiy in 2019 was awarded the Nobel Peace Prize.

The calm was short-lived.

The TPLF, which before Abiy had been the dominant partner in the ruling government coalition, chafed under the new regime. TPLF forces were accused of attacking and looting Ethiopian military bases in November of 2020. Ethiopian troops, aided by forces from Eritrea and militias from the Amhara region, struck back. All parties in the fighting were charged with massive human rights abuses, with Tigrayans suffering most from the violence. As many as 600,000 people, mostly Tigrayans, were estimated to have died, mostly from starvation and disease.

The fighting continued off and on until November 2022 when the African Union helped broker a cease-fire between the Ethiopian government and the TPLF. Soon after the cease-fire, Ethiopian and Tigrayan commanders met in Nairobi, Kenya to negotiate disarming Tigrayan troops and the withdrawal of foreign troops and Amhara militias.

By January 2023 Tigrayan forces had begun to hand in their heavy weapons as the peace process continued. Also, food, medicine and fuel were entering Tigray with increasing regularity.

The peace was fragile, however. Eritrea was not a party to the cease-fire and removal of Eritrean forces was crucial to the settlement. Also, Tigray and the neighboring Amhara region both continued to claim jurisdiction over disputed areas.

Ethiopia: Overview

- Population: 120,812,698 (second most populous in Africa, after Nigeria, 216,746,934)
- Location: Horn of Africa, just north of the equator, near the Red Sea
- Size: 1.6 times the size of Texas
- Official language: Amharic
- Capital: Addis Ababa ("New Flower")
- Religious affiliation: Ethiopian Orthodox, 43%; Muslim, 34%; Protestant, 19% and other, 4%*

- Ethnic representation: Oromo, 35%; Amhara, 26%; Tigray, 6%; Somali, 6% and other, 27%
- Climate: diverse—cool in the mountains of central and northern Ethiopia; rainy and humid in areas of equatorial rain forest in the south and desert-like in parts of northeast, east and southeastern lowlands
- Economy: agriculturally based, with more than 70% of labor force employed in agriculture
- Main export: coffee

For Further Information

Asserate, Asfa-Wossen. "King of Kings: The Triumph and Tragedy of Emperor Haile Selassie I of Ethiopia." Haus Publishing, 2015.

Associated Press. "Ethiopia Orders Full Mobilization." New York Times, October 4, 1935.

"At Long Last, Ethiopia Prepares for Peace Talks." International Crisis Group, July 4, 2022. https://www.crisisgroup.org/africa/horn-africa/ethiopia/long-last-ethiopia-prepares-peace-talks.

"Countries in Africa 2022." World Population Review. https://worldpopulationreview.com/country-rankings/countries-in-africa.

Crummey, Donald Edward. "Ethiopia." Encyclopaedia Britannica, May 20, 2022. https://www.britannica.com/place/Ethiopia.

"Ethiopia: About." Peace Corps. https://www.peacecorps.gov/ethiopia/about/.

"Ethiopia Country Profile." BBC. January 17, 2022. https://www.bbc.com/news/world-africa-13349398.

"Ethiopia in Depth—A Peace Corps Publication." Peace Corps Worldwide. https://peacecorpsworldwide.org/ethiopia-in-depth-a-peace-corps-publication/.

"Ethiopia Profile—Timeline." BBC. October 12, 2020. https://www.bbc.com/news/world-africa-13351397.

Goodwin, Lindsey. "Ethiopian Coffee Culture." The Spruce Eats. September 17, 2020. https://www.thespruceeats.com/ethiopian-coffee-culture-765829.

"Hadar Anthropological and Archaeological Site, Ethiopia." Encyclopedia Britannica. https://www.britannica.com/place/Hadar-anthropological-and-archaeological-site-EthiopiaDATED.

Hocken, Vigdis. "The Ethiopian Calendar." timeanddate.com. https://www.timeanddate.com/calendar/ethiopia-calendar.html

Kapuściński, Ryszard. "The Emperor: Downfall of an Autocrat." Penguin Classics, 2006.

"Meskel, The Ethiopian 'True Cross' Celebration." e-Visa. Ethiopia. https://www.ethiopiaonlinevisa.com/meskel-ethiopian-true-cross-celebration/.

"Population of Cities in Ethiopia (2022)." World Population Review. https://worldpopulationreview.com/countries/cities/ethiopia.

"Queen of Sheba." Encyclopaedia Britannica. https://www.britannica.com/biography/Queen-of-Sheba.

"Rock-Hewn Churches, Lalibela." UNESCO World Heritage Convention. https://whc.unesco.org/en/list/18/.

"U.S. Relations With Ethiopia." United States Department of State. January 14,
    2020. https://www.state.gov/u-s-relations-with-ethiopia/.
Whitman, Alden. "Haile Selassie of Ethiopia Dies at 83." New York Times,
    August 28, 1975.

Afterword

KATHLEEN COSKRAN

WILLIAM HERSHEY'S PEACE Corps reminiscences of teaching in Ethiopia benefit from the ever-moving spyglass of time. The first, written in 1978, came only eight years after his two years as a volunteer and the last, written in 2019, was written 50 years later—testimony, I believe, to the importance of those two years. Hershey and I have never met, but we have had remarkably similar experiences, particularly regarding the lasting effect of our two years teaching in Ethiopia.

I taught in Addis Ababa my first year and, happily, by my second year was transferred to Dilla, a small town in southern Ethiopia, not unlike Hershey's Dabat. There were four Peace Corps volunteers teaching seventh and eighth grade in that small school: Dick, Doug, Claudie, and me. We never challenged another town to a basketball game as Hershey's school did in the second essay, but his run-in with Ato Yohannes reminded me of our great basketball misunderstanding.

Doug was a builder, and, to the students' delight, constructed the first basketball goal in town: the pole, the backboard, and found a ring with a net somewhere that he hung at the proper height. The students swirled around him as he worked, enthusiastic until the very end, when he took an Ethiopian coin out of his pocket and nailed it to the pole—or from the students' point of view, drove a nail through the head of Haile Selassie, who appeared on every coin. According to the students the symbolic impalement of the emperor was a treasonous act.

"Sir," the students said, "you must remove the coin."

"That's ridiculous," Doug said. "I always nail a coin somewhere when I finish a job."

"But, Sir, Sir, you must remove it."

On and on they protested. A couple headed for the local police station. By the time the students recruited me to talk to him, a large crowd had gathered around Doug and the impaled one-cent piece. I reasoned, then pleaded. He refused to remove it. The crowd grew, townspeople as well as students. I like to think it was my influence with him that eventually made him pry the coin off the pole, but it was probably Tafesse, the Ethiopian teacher who shared a house with him, who convinced him to remove the coin, apologize, and save himself, and possibly, the rest of us, from a stoning.

As Hershey observes in "The Outhouse Rebellion," it is so easy for Americans to do the wrong thing.

That story came back to me many years later when I was back in Ethiopia, and I was the American doing the wrong thing. My husband (also a Peace Corps volunteer whom I met in Ethiopia) and I have an Ethiopian foster son, Ahmed, who was a refugee from the horrors that followed the coup that deposed Haile Selassie in 1974. I returned to Ethiopia in 1989 for a number of reasons and was able to spend several days with Ahmed's family, who couldn't do enough for me, especially at mealtimes. Ahmed's father Mohammed spent the entire meal, every meal, insisting that I eat, eat, eat! I did my best, but there were limits. I thought I knew enough about cultural norms to refuse adamantly and repeatedly, but he was relentless, "Eat!" More than once, he tried to put food in my mouth.

On the last day I realized my error. The family, usually with many guests invited to meet me, sat on the floor, around a large carpet that held multiple dishes of wonderful Ethiopian food. Other people eventually leaned against one of the pillows propped against the wall, just out of easy access to the food, and were allowed to stop eating. I stayed frozen in place, sat where I was told to sit. Even though I'd lived in Ethiopia for two years, I hadn't eaten every meal every day with a family, a family who never allowed me to help. It seemed right to stay in the conversation around the wonderful offering of food and drink, until I realized it wasn't.

"Oh, Mohammed," I said, "I see my mistake! I should move *away* from the food when I don't want more to eat." I explained that in my culture we *stay* at the table until everybody has finished eating.

Even with my broken Amharic he understood me.

"Yes," he said. "And you should have been telling me to eat, eat, eat. You should have been offering food to *me* too."

So my only alteration to Hershey's observation on how easy it is for Americans to do the wrong thing would be how

easy it is to assume that the polite or accepted way to do something as simple as entertaining a guest in *your* culture is the
same in *every* culture.

I was a bit taken aback by Hershey's comparison of Donald
Trump to Haile Selassie in his August 9, 2018, column. It is
true that the emperor experienced and expected uncommon
deference. I only saw him in person once, a tiny figure in the
back of a Rolls Royce, trailed by the imperial bodyguard on
motorcycles, going through an Addis Ababa roundabout. At
the first sight of the Rolls, every vehicle in the roundabout,
including the taxi I was in, screeched to a halt, every occupant
leaped out and prostrated themselves on the pavement
because the emperor was passing by. So, yes, Trump would
like that, but Haile Selassie, autocrat that he was, cared about
the future of Ethiopia and eloquently pled for help before the
League of Nations when Italy used chemical warfare—mustard gas—to invade Ethiopia in 1935: "Representatives of the
World, I have come to Geneva to discharge in your midst the
most painful of the duties of the head of a State. What reply
shall I have to take back to my people?" The nations of the
world did nothing, and Ethiopia was occupied by Italy for five
years, but not colonized—an important distinction.

The increase in student protest in a small provincial town
like Dabat was particularly interesting to me. By the time my
future husband Chuck and I left Ethiopia in 1967, student
demonstrations against the emperor were an annual occur-
rence in Addis Ababa. Chuck taught history at Bede Mariam
Lab School at Haile Selassie University in Addis where his
12th-grade students had more information than students in

the provinces, but, he says, not always *accurate* information. His operating philosophy became: "Change is coming, and assuming it's a revolution, let's help it be an intelligent revolution." Students in my little town weren't politicized, but that seems to have changed by the time Hershey arrived in 1968, perhaps inspired by longtime grievances in-country and the student unrest around the world, in France, Germany, the United States and elsewhere. *The times, they were a-changin.'*

I found many similarities to my experiences in his columns, but perhaps what lingers most memorably is how formative those two years were for us both. Hershey and I are still thinking and talking about it more than 50 years later. Those of us lucky enough to spend two or more years living and working in Ethiopia or Nepal or Ukraine know we are simply part of the great human adventure on earth, that there is more than one way to live, love and prosper, plan, hope, and feed a guest.

Kathleen Coskran served as a Peace Corps teacher in Ethiopia from 1965–1967. She is an educator and writer. From 1995–2004 she was principal of the Lake Country School, a large Montessori school in Minnesota. "The High Price of Everything," her short story collection, won a Minnesota Book Award, as did "Tanzania on Tuesday: Writing by American Women Abroad," which she co-edited. She has received several artists' fellowships, including a National Endowment for the Arts Fellowship.

Afterword

ABEBE KIRKOS

MY CLASSMATES AND I first had American Peace Corps teachers in 1967 in Grade 7. Mr. and Mrs. Raymond taught at Dabat Junior Secondary School. Mr. Raymond taught science and Mrs. Raymond taught English. It was thrilling to be taught by teachers whose mother tongue was English.

Both classes were taught in English. They taught at the school on Monday through Friday. The laboratory part of science was taught at their residence on weekends. The science lessons were fascinating because the students were introduced to microscopes and other laboratory items such as test tubes and funnels during biology and chemistry lessons.

The class was also taught American songs like "Do Lord, Oh Do Lord, Oh Do Remember Me" and "Kumbaya" and was introduced to the guitar, which Mr. Raymond played during music class.

The most exciting moment for the students and their parents was on Parents' Day at the end of the school year. Mr. Raymond demonstrated the concept of how an airplane works by flying a model airplane propelled by a mini engine that was tied to a thin, long rope for nearly five minutes.

In 1968 another Peace Corps teacher, Mr. Hershey, was assigned to Dabat. He taught me English in Grade 8. Mr. Hershey was more sociable and livelier than the first Peace Corps teachers. His teaching style was attractive and drew the attention of the class.

He provided lessons in phonetics, dialog and debate. He helped the students learn how to pronounce English words correctly.

He also inculcated the idea of getting a university education in the students' minds. He cited some Ethiopian university students who taught with him as role models. He also inspired us to listen to the BBC and the Voice of America.

Mr. Hershey also offered financial support to some students who were in difficulty. He allowed three students to live with him during his time in Dabat.

Many Americans I met and worked with in Ethiopia were passionate about Ethiopia and regarded it as their second home.

Abebe Kirkos, 67, graduated from a two-year course at the Jimma Teachers Training Institute in Ethiopia and taught for seven years in elementary schools. He later earned a bachelor's degree in statistics from Addis Ababa University and also a post graduate diploma in statistics from Makerere University in Kampala, Uganda. He worked as a statistician in the Ethiopian National Statistical Office for 30 years and is now retired. He is married and lives in Addis Ababa.

Acknowledgments

ALTHOUGH I DIDN'T know it at the time, the idea for this book began taking shape more than 50 years ago when I accepted an invitation to become a Peace Corps volunteer in Ethiopia.

My partner on this half-century journey has been my wife Marcia, also a Peace Corps volunteer in Ethiopia. We served in neighboring towns and married after returning to the United States. Our shared experiences and memories provided the material for these Peace Corps tales.

Thanks to Marcia for helping keep those memories alive and for her continued support and encouragement.

Thanks, too, to our kids, Laura and Patrick, for listening over and over to our Peace Corps stories and maybe even learning from them a lesson or two about what a fascinating and challenging place the world and all the people in it are.

Marcia, Laura and Patrick all deserve credit for sticking with me through the ups, downs, twists and turns of a newspaper reporter's career.

That career allowed me to turn those Peace Corps memories into the stories in this book. I'm grateful to the newspapers—the Akron Beacon Journal and the Dayton Daily News—that hired me, found the space for these stories and then gave permission for them to be reprinted.

Special thanks at the Beacon Journal goes to two former editors of the Beacon, the paper's former Sunday magazine. Ann Sheldon Mezger and the late William Bierman agreed to run the stories on a squabble about cleaning the school bathroom, a basketball game that nearly turned into an international incident and a refugee's brave journey from war-torn Ethiopia, through the Sudan, and finally to the United States.

Special thanks, too, to Michael Douglas, the Beacon Journal's retired editorial page editor. Michael generously agreed to publish the commentaries reflecting on my Peace Corps experience that I wrote after retiring.

Only one of the book's stories first appeared in the Dayton Daily News, but that understates the debt I owe to that paper. I left the newspaper business briefly in the mid-1990s, and it was the Daily News that gave me the opportunity to return in 1999. More than a decade of reporting for the Daily News provided the momentum to keep writing in retirement and ultimately to put the book together.

This project wouldn't have been possible without the support and encouragement I received growing up from my late parents, Josephine and Clark Hershey. They were always there to help, in person or through the letters and taped messages they sent when I was 8,000 miles away in Ethiopia.

I grew up and went to school in Flint, Michigan, when Flint was a boomtown with 80,000 General Motors employees. The economic and racial diversity of the Flint public schools gave me an early start in learning how to get along with people from different backgrounds, a lesson that helped me in Dabat, the small town where I taught school for two years.

The professors at Albion College in Michigan, where I received my undergraduate degree, opened my eyes and mind to the injustices and inequality in the United States and the world and the opportunities to do something about them.

My Peace Corps' experience wouldn't have been possible without the acceptance I received from Ethiopians in Dabat and across the country.

The school director, Demoz, went out of his way to make me feel welcome and the faculty usually treated me like a colleague, not a ferenji. I still remember most of the teachers by name—Shumbeza, Bahru, Girma, Mitiku, Abraham, Mesfin, Yidege, Asmamaw, Dagnew, Demissie, Kebede, Yekalo, Maaza, Zewditu, Laaka, Ambachew, Mohammed and Alemante.

The students were the reason I was sent to Dabat. They came to school eager and thankful to learn. The three students who lived with me over two years—Alebachew, Sisay and Abraham—helped with household chores and kept me from cross-cultural blunders.

The Peace Corps friends I made in Ethiopia helped keep alive the memories that went into this book. Susan and Roger

Whitaker have been family friends for more than 50 years. I met Rick Stoner when my Peace Corps experience started, and he gave Marcia and me a chance to return to Ethiopia in 1973 for a training program he directed. Rich Casey always had a place for me to stay during visits to Addis Ababa. The late Ned Roberts provided hospitality during my occasional stops in Gondar, the biggest city close to Dabat. Ned also helped Marcia and me welcome Ethiopian refugees resettling in Ohio. The late Gwen Hudson, Marcia's housemate in Ethiopia, was an outstanding volunteer and good friend.

This is the fourth book I've written for The University of Akron Press, and I'm grateful for the editors' skill in turning manuscripts into finished projects.

John C. Green, director emeritus of the university's Bliss Institute of Applied Politics, was a coauthor of one book and provided encouragement on the other three.

Thanks, too, to former Ohio governors Richard F. Celeste and Bob Taft, Kathleen Coskran, a former Ethiopian Peace Corps volunteer, and my former student Abebe Kirkos for their contributions to this book. Kathleen also provided valuable advice on how to share with readers my Peace Corps experience in a country with thousands of years of history. Her superb editing skills helped iron out rough spots in the book.

William Hershey spent more than 40 years reporting on Ohio politics and government at the local, state and national levels. He was the Washington correspondent for the Akron Beacon Journal and Columbus Bureau Chief for the Beacon Journal and the Dayton Daily News. He is the author of three other books: "Mr. Chairman: The Life and Times of Ray C. Bliss" (with John C. Green); "Quick & Quotable: Columns from Washington, 1985–1997" and "Profiles in Achievement: The Gifts, Quirks and Foibles of Ohio's Best Politicians" (with colleagues). He was a major contributor to coverage that won the 1987 Pulitzer Prize for the Beacon Journal staff for reporting on Sir James Goldsmith's attempted takeover of the Goodyear Tire & Rubber Company.

Printed in the United States
by Baker & Taylor Publisher Services